Contemporary Fiqh

Detailed and Elaborative Articles on Contemporary Fiqhi Issues

Edited by
Shaykh Mufti Saiful Islām

JKN Publications

© Copyright by JKN Publications

First Published in May 2019

ISBN 978-1-909114-45-6

British Library Cataloguing in Publication Data
A catalogue record for this book is available from the British Library.

All Rights Reserved. No part of this book may be reproduced, stored in a retrieval system or transmitted in any form or by any means, electronic, mechanical, photocopying, recording or otherwise, without the prior permission of the copyright owner.

Publisher's Note:

Every care and attention has been put into the production of this book. If however, you find any errors it is our own, for which we seek Allāh's ﷻ forgiveness and reader's pardon.

Published by:

JKN Publications
118 Manningham Lane
Bradford
West Yorkshire
BD8 7JF
United Kingdom

t: +44 (0) 1274 308 456 | w: www.jkn.org.uk | e: info@jkn.org.uk

Book Title: Contemporary Fiqh

Author: Shaykh Mufti Saiful Islām

"In the Name of Allāh, the Most Beneficent, the Most Merciful"

Contents

Introduction.. 5

Prayer of an Ill Person................................. 7

Acceptance of Du'a..................................... 22

Ramadhān Fast for a Diabetic Person.................. 25

Three Simultaneous Divorces in One Sitting........... 35

Right of Custody of the Child after Divorce............ 44

Women Exercising in her Home......................... 50

Treatment for Hair loss................................. 52

Women and Nutrition.................................. 55

Becoming a Female Doctor-What are My Limitations?.......... 60

Hijab from Non-Mahram in-Laws....................... 65

Organ Transplantation and Blood Transfusion.......... 73

Islamic Perspective of Abortion....................... 89

Medicine and Food Containing Haram Ingredients... 95

Sterilisation.. 112

Caesarean... 115

Swine Flu Vaccine.................................... 117

Smoking Shīsha....................................... 124

Planning for a Baby.................................. 143

Depression... 147

Chronic Depression.................................. 150

Autism... 156

Sleeping Problems.................................... 161

Cupping-Hijāmah..................................... 172

Sending Dead Relatives Abroad for Burial.............. 177

Isāl-e-Thawāb (Sending Reward to the Deceased)........ 182

Introduction

In the name of Allāh the Most Gracious and the Most Merciful
All Praises belong to Allāh the Lord of the Worlds and may His Infinite Salutations and
Blessings be bestowed upon His Final Messenger, his pure family, noble Companions ﷺ
and those who follow their path until the Final Day.

Alhamdulillāh, being privileged to work under the supervision of Shaykh Mufti Saiful Islām Sāhib for a significant number of years in serving the JKN Fatawa department full-time and contributing to many JKN publications like the *Ask A Mufti (3 volumes), Should I follow a Madhab, Marriage a Complete Solution* to name but a few, not to exclude this one in your hands and also granting me the opportunity to lecture on Fiqh such as *Al-Hidayah* (a renowned classical juridical manual of the Hanafi Madhab) and Hadīth and other various subjects, is due to Allāh's ﷺ Divine Mercy and Favours upon me. I cannot express my sincere appreciation to Shaykh Mufti Saiful Islām as much as he rightfully deserves other than to pray for his success and acceptance in both worlds for his endeavours and relentless efforts in preserving the Dīn especially in the current climate.

This book is a selection of detailed *Fiqhi* (juridical) articles taken from our recent publication, *Ask A Mufti.* These detailed articles provide an in depth and elaborative response to some of the queries posted to us in our Fatawa department over the last decade. The topics discussed range between purity, domestic issues, Halāl and Harām, Islamic medical ethics, marital issues, rituals and so forth. Many of the juristic cases are retrospectively unprecedented, as a result of the ongoing societal changes and new issues arising.

Contemporary Fiqh　　　　　　　　　　Introduction

To respond to the newly emerging issues is the necessary role of the Ulama in the field of research to provide detailed Islamic guidelines for the masses because much of them inevitably effect the spiritual component of the day to day Muslim living. This is to ensure Muslims do not infringe any of the Islamic principles in respect to the new contemporary issues that effect them. This illustrates that Islām acknowledges the change of times and circumstances and provides guiding principles for them. To extrapolate those legal principles and apply them to modern times can only be accomplished by the Ulama in the field of research, e.g. Muftis.

There are in total a collection of twenty-five *Fiqhi* articles in this book. We soon hope to add more articles in the near future when publishing the second volume. Those articles pertaining to medical ethics have been contributed by Maulāna Dr Rafāqat Rashid whilst the others either by Mufti Abdul Waheed and Shaykh Mufti Saiful Islām. All the articles have been thoroughly checked and endorsed by Mufti Sāhib himself.

We hope this becomes a useful source of information for those Ulama and inquisitive brothers and sisters who wish to seek Islamic guidelines on these particular matters and we pray Allāh ﷻ accepts the efforts of Shaykh Mufti Saiful Islām and of those who have contributed to this work, Amīn.

(Mufti) Abdul Waheed
Teacher of Fiqh at Jāmiah Khātamun Nabiyyeen
May 2019/Ramadhān 1440

Prayer of an ill Patient and Some Rules of Purity
Dr Rafaqat Rashid

Q Could you please elaborate on the Islamic rulings pertaining to the prayer of an ill patient and purity? Many patients in hospitals tend to seek advice from those that do not have adequate knowledge of Islām. I have witnessed many patients either not following the correct Islamic rules regarding this matter or neglect their Salāh altogether. I feel it is necessary that this issue is addressed to the general masses. As you are someone from a medical profession as well as an Islamic Scholar, I would be very appreciative if you could shed some light on this matter in great detail.

A Being someone from the medical profession, I see ill people virtually everyday. Most of the patients I deal with are Muslims. This has given me an insight into the habits and practices of Muslims, regarding issues related to ritual purity and Salāh (prayer) when they are unwell. It is quite unfortunate that a lot of ignorance exists amongst Muslims regarding issues of ritual purity and prayer, during times when they may be sick and not able to perform these forms of worship as they usually do. What saddens me the most is that some people are particular about their Salāh when fit and healthy, but can be quite negligent when unwell.

There may be a number of reasons for this. It may be that because of their illness, their clothes or body are thought to be impure and because they have difficulty performing Wudhu (ablution) or Ghusl (bath), they are unsatisfied that Tayammum (dry ablution) is

Contemporary Fiqh

Prayer of an Ill Person

sufficient enough to purify them. As a result they miss their Salāh and thus, make it Qadhā.

There have been occasions when I have witnessed practicing Muslims who are punctual with their Salāh and because of their unfortunate illness, their mind may be clouded and unfocussed, or they are not fully attentive to time or slightly disorientated of time. Because of this reason, their Salāh time has passed by though, if they were told of the Salāh time and prompted, they would have performed it. Their carers or relatives, out of concern for the patient's health, deliberately do not inform them of the Salāh time. Even if the patient had expressed his desire to read Salāh, they usually brush aside the issue hoping he will forget or realise that it would be too difficult (i.e. how will you do Wudhu or Tayammum? How will you change your clothes as they are impure? Where is the Qiblah and how will you face it?) The truth is that they could be imposing sin on the patient as well as themselves by doing this. This act is of no real benefit to the patient nor to themselves. If the patient died in this state then who would carry the responsibility?

Some patients take certain advice from doctors regarding prayer and as a result abstain from prayer completely. It is important that they consult the Ulamā regarding this and act upon those concessions that the Shari'ah has allowed for those who have difficulty. Salāh should not be considered a burden but rather a means of comfort and solace.

Sayyidunā Abū Uthmān ☙ narrates, "I was with Salmān ☙ under a tree. He held on to a branch which was dry and shook it until all the leaves had fallen. He then said, 'O, Abū Uthmān! Will you not ask me why I am doing this?' I replied, 'Why are you doing this?' He said, 'This is what the Holy Prophet ﷺ did when I was with him under a tree; he held on to a branch which was dry and shook it until all the leaves had fallen. He then said, 'O, Salmān! Will you not ask me why I am doing this?' I replied, 'Why are you doing this?' He remarked, 'Verily, when a Muslim makes Wudhu properly and then observes his Salāh five times a day, his sins fall off just as these leaves have fallen off.' He then recited the following verse of the Holy Qur'ān, **"Establish Salāh at the two ends of the day, and during portions of the night. Verily, good deeds cancel ill deeds. This is a reminder for the mindful." (11:114)"**

Illness is a reminder of our vulnerability and reminds us of death. It is for this reason that we should be even more cautious that we are performing our Salāh the right way, if at all. Salāh is a mercy for the believer. It is a time when an ill person's sins are purified because of the patience a sick person endures whilst suffering. It is a time when the help of Allāh ﷻ is truly needed. **"Seek Allāh's help with patience and Salāh." (2:24)**

Sayyidunā Abū Saeed ﷺ narrates that the Holy Prophet ﷺ said, "Whenever a Muslim suffers from an affliction, disease, grief or anguish, or even a thorn-prick, he is forgiven by Allāh ﷻ on that account." (Bukhāri)

It is for this reason that I have decided to write this article. I hope Inshā-Allāh that I am able to cover most of the questions that arise in dealing with purity and the prayer of the ill, in an easy to understand fashion. I have used my knowledge and experience of the hospital environment and medical scenarios to place a clear picture and pull out practical points on how one should deal with this issue. I pray that it is of some use. I will begin by discussing Tahārah (purification), and the Ma'zūr patient and I will finish on the Salāh of the Marīdh (ill), including the subject of compensatory Fidyah.

Tahārah (Ritual Purity) & the Ill

There are some patients who leave Salāh because they find purifying their body and clothes a difficult task. This is quite common in a hospital setting when the patient is alone on the ward, he speaks poor English and is either too embarrassed to express his concern to the nurses, or feels that the burden of cleaning himself is too much to bear. For this reason, they leave their Salāh because they believe that Salāh is not valid without purifying the body and clothes. This belief is wrong and should be discussed with the Ulamā if there is a doubt. The Salāh of such a person will be valid in situations where performing Wudhu/Ghusl causes serious agony, where there is fear of the illness worsening as a result of ablution, or where there are genuinely no alternate clothes available to wear. It may be possible that another hospital gown is available on enquiry which is pure for prayer. Laziness or being embarrassed is no excuse in Sharī'ah.

Here is an example: If a patient is wearing clothes which are impure and by placing anything underneath him, it also immediately becomes impure, then he should read his Salāh in this state because they are considered pure for him as he is excused. If by re-

Contemporary Fiqh   Prayer of an Ill Person

moving his clothes or by the cloth placed underneath him, he suffers pain or his illness becomes worse, then he can read Salāh in this state, regardless of whether the newly placed cloth becomes impure if placed under him.

(Raddul Muhtār alā Durrul Mukhtār, vol.1 pg. 507)

Rulings of Wudhu on those Parts of the Body which are Injured

I find that a lot of ignorance exists in the issue of plaster casts, bandages and even simple plasters. Some people excuse themselves from Wudhu and thus Salāh, with the belief that it will not be valid if they have a splint or bandage on their arm etc. There are also those who, out of laziness, refuse to take off a simple dressing and thus have not purified themselves with Wudhu properly. Rather they are reading Salāh without Wudhu and such a Salāh is not acceptable. To clarify this matter, one needs to remember a few rules! If any part of the body which is normally washed etc. as part of the Wudhu, is broken, wounded or bandaged, then there are three rulings relating to this:

1. If removing the bandage proves difficult or is injurious, or washing that limb is injurious, then Masah (wiping) should be performed, if this act is not harmful. The Masah should be done on the whole bandage, even if the bandage is beyond the wounded area. If Masah also proves to be harmful, then this limb area should be left and the Wudhu will be acceptable.

2. If removing the bandage is not injurious but putting the bandage on again proves difficult by oneself and there is no assistant

| Contemporary Fiqh | Prayer of an Ill Person |

easily accessible who could do this for the patient, then Masah may be performed on top of the bandage.

3. If removing the bandage is not injurious nor putting the bandage on again is difficult, then if there is no harm in washing the affected limb, this limb must be washed. If the wound area may be harmed by washing, then just the wound area should be spared and the rest of the limb washed. The wound area should be wiped if this is not injurious, otherwise left alone.

If a bandage is wrapped around a wound and blood or pus is visible on the outer surface of the bandage and this is such that if the bandage was not wrapped, then this blood or pus would have flowed from there, then the Wudhu will be broken.

The above rulings of injury/bandage also apply to Ghusl.
(Durrul Mukhtār, vol.1 pg. 42-43)

Allāh ﷻ explains that He does not want to place a burden on us regarding purifying ourselves for Salāh. Tayammum (dry ablution) is a blessing from Allāh ﷻ especially for those who are ill and find it difficult to perform Wudhu.

"O you who believe! When you come to offer Salāh (prayer), wash your faces and your hands (forearms) up to the elbows, rub (by passing wet hands over) your heads, and (wash) your feet up to the ankles. If you are in a state of Janābah (e.g. had a sexual discharge), purify yourselves (wash your whole body). However, if you are ill, or on a journey, or any of you arrive from answer-

ing the call of nature, or you have been in contact with women (i.e. sexual intercourse) and you find no water, then perform Tayammum with clean earth and rub with it your faces and hands. Allāh does not want to place you in difficulty, but He wants to purify you, and to complete His favour on you that you may be thankful." (5:6)

One can only appreciate a blessing when he understands when and how that blessing is a benefit. Unfortunately, Tayammum is one of those blessings which is poorly understood. Tayammum can be done on a wall, small rock/stone or even on a table surface with slight dust on it.

Unfortunately, there are those who perform Tayammum in situations where performing Wudhu requires no real effort but because they consider themselves sick, they feel this would be acceptable. This is a grave mistake. Then there are those who are at the other extreme and no matter how seriously ill they may be, they will not accept performing Tayammum as the acceptable method of purification. Rather, they prefer to undergo serious difficulty in performing ablution causing themselves agony and pain and worsening their illness. The truth of the matter is, that this is also wrong as it expresses the non-acceptance of the blessings of ease that Allāh ﷻ has ordained for moments of difficulty. It is considered careless and not being considerate of Allāh's ﷻ commands. It is rather, following ones desires and what one prefers to do. Just like Wudhu is a command from Allāh ﷻ so is Tayammum.

So when is it Acceptable for Someone to Perform Tayammum as a Patient?

If water is required for purity (Wudhu/Ghusl) and

1. There is fear of the illness becoming worse,
2. There is delayed recovery as a result of using water, or
3. If the person is well but there is fear of him becoming ill on using water (i.e. use of cold water).

If the patient is incapable of getting the water to purify himself, or unable to perform Wudhu (i.e. his illness becomes worse if he attempts it), or if there is no one to assist him in performing Wudhu with water, then it would be permissible for the patient to do Tayammum instead.

The above should be acted upon through good judgement, through genuine experience and in some cases through the explicit advice of a practicing qualified Muslim doctor (i.e. to abstain from Wudhu/Ghusl). (Raddul Muhtār, Vol. 1 pg.397)

What if the patient has amputated limb parts? That person whose hands and feet are amputated should pour water on his limbs if possible, when washing for Wudhu. If he is unable to do this then he should do Tayammum. If the hands are wounded, or a part of or the whole of the hand has been amputated and it is not possible to pour water on the face, then the face should be wiped on the earth or wall with the intention of Tayammum. If the face is wounded and it is not possible to do even this, then he may perform Salāh without purification (i.e. Wudhu/Tayammum). (Ahsanul Fatāwa, Vol. 2 pg. 17)

That person whose feet are amputated, up to or above the ankle, or whose hands are amputated, up to or above the wrist, then he may pray Salāh without Wudhu/Tayammum and this is sufficient for him (i.e. there is no need for him to do Qadhā). If his hands are not amputated up to or beyond the wrist and if there is someone to assist him, then it is Wājib for him to perform Wudhu, otherwise not.

Definition of Ma'zūr
Ma'zūr is he who undergoes an illness or state, where he is continuously subjected to uncontrollable Hadath (i.e. an act of impurity that breaks Wudhu e.g. continuously dribbling urine) and this Hadath encompasses the full time of that prescribed Fardh Salāh, to the extent that he is unable to find any time within this Salāh time to perform Wudhu and pray Salāh, having been cleared from that Hadath (impurity). For example, he is dribbling urine or passing wind continuously and is unable to perform Wudhu and read Salāh in this allocated Salāh time. (Durrul Mukhtār, pg. 45)

If a person dribbles urine but not to the extent that it lasts throughout the whole time of that Salāh and finds that he has sufficient time to do Wudhu and perform his Salāh, then he is not Ma'zūr. He must wait until the dribbling ceases and then perform Wudhu and read Salāh.

If during Salāh there is a doubt or fear that he has dribbled then he should break his Salāh and see whether this is the case. If he has dribbled then he must wash the affected area, change to clean clothes if needed and perform his Wudhu and Salāh again. If however, there is no sign of dribble, then he should not entertain such

Contemporary Fiqh	Prayer of an Ill Person

doubt but rather, place a tissue sprinkled with a little water around the area. This will help in preventing him having such doubts.

If the Hadath presents itself after the beginning time of Fardh Salāh (and some of the Salāh time has passed and the full time has not been encompassed), then he should wait until the last few moments of this Salāh period. If the Hadath does not cease then he should perform Wudhu and read Salāh in this state. If the Hadath ceased within the Salāh time, then the Salāh performed should be repeated (i.e. he is not a Ma'zūr). However, if the Hadath encompasses up until the end of the Salāh time then he does not need to repeat the Salāh because he is a Ma'zūr.

(Raddul Muhtār, Vol.1, pg. 397)

Rulings for Ma'zūr

A Ma'zūr should renew his Wudhu for every Salāh time and having clean clothes, if possible, read any of his Fardh, Sunnah and/or Nafl Salāh in that time. As long as that Salāh time is not finished, the Hadath (i.e. dribbling of urine) will not break his Wudhu. However, other Nawāqidh (breakers of Wudhu) will break his Wudhu. If for one whole Salāh period, the dribbling has continued and he is unable to perform Wudhu and read Salāh (i.e. becomes Ma'zūr), then it is not a condition for this dribbling to persist throughout the next Salāh period. Rather, if he dribbles only once throughout this period, then that is sufficient for him to remain Ma'zūr. If a whole Salāh time passes and he has had no dribbling at all, then he no longer remains Ma'zūr. (Durrul Mukhtār, pg.45)

Contemporary Fiqh   Prayer of an Ill Person

If in the state of Salāh the clothes become damp because of the dribbling, then in the state of Ma'zūr this will be forgiven (i.e. he does not need to wash them to remain pure for this Salāh).

(Durrul Mukhtār, pg. 45)

Method of Praying Salāh When Sitting
There are some patients who sit and read Salāh even though they have the strength to stand. This is not permissible. If there is a sick person who is unable to fulfil all the Arkān (essentials) of Salāh, then he must pray according to what his strength and ability allows him. If by standing;

- There is a strong possibility of him falling/collapsing or becoming dizzy,
- he suffers injury or severe pain when standing,
- his illness may worsen or the recovery is delayed,
- he is physically unable to stand because of disability,
- or his Wudhu may become nullified (i.e. he has urinary incontinence and if he stands it is likely that he will begin to dribble urine), then in any of the above circumstances, he does not need to stand and pray. Rather, he sits and prays and performs Ruku by bowing his head. He should sit in the Tashahhud position, if possible, otherwise, any position that allows him ease in performing the Salāh. (Raddul Muhtār, Vol.2, pg.566-567)

If it is possible for him to stand for a short while to pray, then he should begin his Salāh in such a manner and try to stand as long as he is able to, even though this may be for a short time (i.e. the time taken for him to do his Takbīr Tahrīmah (initial Takbīr)). This

Contemporary Fiqh   Prayer of an Ill Person

point is essential because it may invalidate his Salāh. Even if it means that he rests on a stick, pillar or another person. (Raddul Muhtār, Vol.2, pg.567)

If someone genuinely finds it difficult to remain standing for prolonged periods because of weakness, pain etc. in Salāh (e.g. Tarāwīh), then he may rest on a wall, pillar, walking stick etc. This is not considered Makrūh and can be quite common in the aged. There are some patients who are sound of mind but whilst reading Salāh they express their agony with clear words of moaning such as Ah!, Ouch! etc. and are quite unmindful of this. It is important to know that if a patient is of sound mind and makes these noises during Salāh, his Salāh will be void and will need repeating. (Tahtāwi pg. 324)

If someone becomes unwell whilst reading Salāh standing up, then he may read the rest of the Salāh sitting or lying with what is most appropriate for him, regarding his illness. If he is unwell and he is praying whilst sitting or lying and he has gained the strength to sit or stand whilst reading Salāh, then he must stand and continue his Salāh as long as he did not perform Ruku and Sajdah with gesture.

If someone is dressed in such a way that his 'Awra (parts of body that should be covered in Salāh) is not fully covered on standing but is on sitting, then he must sit and pray. Similarly, if someone who, on standing because of the burden, is unable to do his Qirāt (recitation) properly because of exhaustion or breathlessness, then he should sit and read Salāh. (Raddul Muhtār, Vol.2, pg. 565)

Contemporary Fiqh   Prayer of an Ill Person

If he is not able to perform Ruku and Sajdah, even though he is able to stand, then he should sit and pray and signal with his head for Ruku (by bowing his head) and bow further with his head for Sajdah. If he can stand and do Sajdah but cannot perform Ruku, then he must stand, signal for Ruku by bowing as far as he can and then perform Sajdah. If by performing Sajdah his wound begins to flow but not whilst sitting, then he should signal for Sajdah with his head. To bring something to the forehead on which to do Sajdah is Makrūh Tahrīmi but if one places something on the floor which raises the platform for his forehead to rest during Sajdah, then this is permissible. (Raddul Muhtār, Vol.2, pg. 567)

Method of Praying Salāh When Lying

If someone is unable to even sit because of lack of ability or strength, whilst even resting on something or someone, then he must lie and pray his Salāh by signalling. The most preferable way to lie down is to lie on the back facing the feet towards the Qiblah and placing a cushion or pillow to raise the head, so that the person is able to look in the direction of Qiblah. It would also be permissible for him to lie on his right or left but facing the Qiblah. If one is able, then he must signal with his head for Ruku and Sajdah (bowing for Sajdah should be more than for Ruku). Signalling with eyes or eyebrows will not be permissible.

(Durrul Mukhtār pg.101-102)

If the above is not possible, then the patient should read in a way which is of ease for him. If there is no one to assist him in facing the Qiblah, then it is sufficient for him to read in the direction which is appropriate at that time.

Those Exempted From Performing Salāh

If someone is unable to perform Salāh even by signalling with their head, then he should not read Salāh but rather, make Qadhā of this Salāh. If this state exists for the duration of five Salāhs or more, then there is no need for him to do Qadhā of the missed Salāhs. This also applies if he can only read Salāh by signalling with his eyebrows/eyelids or by heart intention, even if he is fully aware and conscious.

If someone has obvious difficulty remembering which Rak'at they are in because of their illness, then to perform Salāh at that time is not necessary. Rather, he should do Qadhā of these Salāhs. However, if someone repeatedly reminds him, then this is permissible. This is the same ruling for the patient who is old and has poor/deficient memory. If there is no one to remind him about the number of Rak'at he has prayed, then he may read according to what he thinks is the most correct.

State of Unconsciousness

If the patient has been completely unconscious for more than five consecutive Salāhs, in this state those Salāhs are forgiven and it is not obligatory to do Qadhā. If it is less than five Salāhs, he will have to pray his Qadhā. This rule also applies to that patient who has become mentally insane and has no insight. If however, the patient is semi-conscious and he is unable to perform those Salāhs (he will be forgiven for this), but as soon as he is fully conscious again he will have to do Qadhā of these missed prayers.

(Raddul Muhtār, Vol.2, pg. 583-584)

Contemporary Fiqh — Prayer of an Ill Person

He will need to do Wasiyyah (make a will) of Fidyah (monetary compensation) for these Qadhā Salāhs if he has not prayed them and he dies.

If however, he is slightly sedated/drowsy or in varied consciousness as a result of taking medication and is not able to focus, then he must do Qadhā of his missed Salāhs, if he is unable to perform them. This is because the act of taking medication is voluntary like when sleeping and for such an act, the missed Salāhs have to be read as Qadhā. Similarly, if he has taken medication and became unconscious with this, then he must perform Qadhā for missed prayers as this is of his own doing. (Durrul Mukhtār pg. 102)

Allāh ﷻ Knows Best

Acceptance of Du'ā

Q What does it mean that Allāh ﷻ accepts every Du'ā we make? I have been doing Du'ā for a particular matter but it seems that it is not getting accepted?

A From the Ahādīth we understand that Du'ās are accepted in one of the following three ways:

1. The request (of the person making Du'ā) is fulfilled in this world,
2. The Du'ā is stored as a treasure (for the benefit of the person making it) in the Hereafter,
3. Due to the Du'ā, a difficulty or a calamity is averted (in proportion to the request made in the Du'ā).

The Ādāb of Du'ā are:

1. To ensure that one is in a state of cleanliness.
2. To be in the state of Wudhu
3. To face towards the Qiblah.
4. To do some good action before making Du'ā (i.e. giving charity or performing Salāh or making Dhikr).
5. To sit while making Du'ā as one sits in the Tashahhud posture.
6. To raise ones hands (when making Du'ā) with a slight gap between them.
7. To glorify Allāh ﷻ and say His praises in the beginning.
8. To recite Durūd and Salām (i.e. to send salutations upon the beloved Prophet ﷺ).

| Contemporary Fiqh | Acceptance of Du'ā |

9. To focus exclusively towards Allāh ﷻ whilst making Du'ā and to have firm belief that only Allāh ﷻ can answer his Du'ā.
10. To beg and implore Allāh ﷻ with humility.
11. Whilst making Du'ā, both the words and the body posture should be such as to demonstrate total humility, meekness and piety. Ones voice should also be soft.
12. Not to look towards the sky when making Du'ā.
13. Not to adopt a singing tone or poetic language in Du'ā.
14. To admit and confess ones sins. Care should be taken that one does not mention ones specific sins when making Du'ā jointly with others. However, one can say in general terms e.g. O' Allāh ﷻ, forgive all our sins, major and minor. However, when making Du'ā individually, one can recollect ones past sins and then ask and beg Allāh's ﷻ forgiveness for each sin specifically and to make Du'ā from the bottom of ones heart with the strongest presence of mind and firm belief that Allāh ﷻ shall accept.
15. One can repeat each Du'ā at least three times.
16. To cry whilst making Du'ā and if one cannot cry, then one should emulate the act of crying.
17. Not to make Du'ā for impossible things (e.g. make me young again).
18. When making Du'ā for someone else, firstly Du'ā should be made for oneself and then for others.
19. To use the Du'ās of the Qur'ān and Ahādīth.
20. To turn to Allāh ﷻ in every need, whether big or small, even when in need of something as minor as a shoe lace.

Contemporary Fiqh	Acceptance of Du'ā

21. If one is an Imām, then the Du'ā should be made in the plural form to include the congregation and not in the singular.
22. Before concluding the Du'ā, to again glorify Allāh ﷻ and to say His praises, then...
23. to recite Durūd Sharīf and then...
24. to say Āmīn.
25. Lastly wipe the hands over the face.
26. When Du'ās are answered, the Holy Prophet ﷺ has taught us to express our appreciation by saying:

اَلْحَمْدُ لِلّٰهِ الَّذِيْ بِعِزَّتِهِ وَجَلَالِهِ تَتِمُّ الصَّالِحَاتُ

Alhamdulillāhil-Ladhī Bi'izzatihī Wa Jalālihī Tatimmus Sālihāt

Trans: Praise be to Allāh ﷻ that good works have been accomplished by His Power and Glory.

Allāh ﷻ Knows Best

Ramadhān Fast for a Diabetic Person

Dr Rafaqat Rashid

Q My father is a diabetic who takes insulin injections and insists on fasting. His doctor has told him not to fast but my father insists that he should fast without informing the doctor. He did this last year and kept most of the fasts. What advise would you give?

A I sympathise with your father as I do with all the Muslim patients, who wish to fast during Ramadhān and taste the virtues that Allāh ﷻ has blessed the Muslims with during this great holy month. Unfortunately, just like any form of act, if the act becomes too demanding, then one is only causing themselves injury and preventing themselves carrying out that act, or similar acts, effectively again.

One thing is for sure that Allāh ﷻ does not burden a soul more than what it can bear. **"On no soul does Allāh place a burden greater than it can bear"** (2:286). Whether he has a chronic illness or is a traveller, if it proves too difficult for the person concerned to carry out that task, then he/she is exempt from that duty.

"Ramadhān is the (month) in which was sent down the Qur'ān, as a guide to mankind, also clear (signs) for guidance and judgement (between right and wrong). So whoever among you witnesses the month should fast in it, but if any one is ill, or on a journey, the prescribed period (should be made up) by days later. Allāh desires ease for you; He does not want to put you to

difficulties. (He wants you) to complete the prescribed period and to glorify Him in that He has guided you; and perchance you shall be grateful." (2:185)

- The Muslim jurists have agreed that fasting is not obligatory upon children and those people who are incapable of fasting due to;
- Old age (frail)
- Chronic disease (e.g. diabetes, chronic lung problems like bronchitis, chronic heart disease, chronic kidney disease or any chronic debilitating illness.
- Any acute illness or injury where it would be harmful for the person to fast (one makes up the days missed at an alternative time)
- Pregnant or nursing mothers (one makes up the days missed at an alternative time)
- Menstruating women or women with post-natal bleeding (one makes up the days missed at an alternative time)
- Travellers (one makes up the days missed at an alternative time)

Fasting during Ramadhān is an important form of worship. Fasting is a prescription from Allāh ﷻ which encourages self-discipline, self-restraint and generosity. It also reminds us of the suffering of the poor, who may rarely get to eat well. It is a time when Allāh ﷻ opens up His doors of Mercy to His servants.

Such great reward and blessings are only deserved when the servant has to bear patiently with what Allāh ﷻ has prescribed. This

| Contemporary Fiqh | Ramadhān Fast for a Diabetic Person |

blessed month requires us to change our normal daily habits by altering our meal times and daily routine, devoting more time in ones worship and use of certain traditional foods. This can have a major impact on our biological diet and timing, which requires our body to adjust to these demands. It is this biological adjustment which can be potentially dangerous for those who are ill.

As a Muslim, you must be aware that Islām permits leniency and if you have diabetes, you are **not obliged to fast if it will affect your health**. However, if for whatever reason, you choose to observe the fast and you are taking medication for your diabetes, such as sulphonlyureas (for example gliclazide) or insulin, you will need to discuss this with your diabetes team. In many cases, your diabetes nurse or doctor will be able to make recommendations regarding your treatment (such as dose reduction/change of timings of medication etc), that will allow you to fast but keep you safe.

Generally speaking, the longer the hours of daylight, the longer the period of fasting and this may cause some difficulties in maintaining your blood sugars. If you do not discuss medication changes and commence fasting, you may be at risk of **hypoglycaemia (low blood sugar)**.

The way that you need to manage your diabetes during Ramadhān will depend on the type of treatment you have for your diabetes. According to the treatment received, people with diabetes can be divided into three groups.

Contemporary Fiqh | Ramadhān Fast for a Diabetic Person

1. DIET ONLY

If you belong to this group, then you must fast and continue with your normal healthy diet and avoid over eating. People who are overweight who manage their diabetes by diet alone, may reduce their weight by fasting, providing that they do not break their fast with high fat high/calorie foods. This may lead to better control of diabetes.

2. DIET AND ORAL TABLETS

If you belong to this group, you can also fast if your diabetes control is good. You will probably have to continue with your usual healthy diet and in addition, follow the advice given below about your tablets.

a) One daily dose in the morning e.g. Metformin. If you are taking only one dose of oral tablets in the morning normally, then you should continue with the same dose in Ramadhān, BUT the tablet should now be taken at the time of Iftār (breaking fast) instead of the morning.

b) Two daily doses (morning and evening). If you are usually on twice daily doses, you should continue to take these two tablets during Ramadhān. You may need to make changes in the timing and quantity of tablets taken in the following ways;

i. The morning tablets taken on normal days should now be taken at the time of Iftār (breaking fast) at dusk. The dose will remain the same.

ii. The evening dose is taken at the time of closing your fast at Suhūr (dawn) but reduce this dose to half your usual evening

| Contemporary Fiqh | Ramadhān Fast for a Diabetic Person |

dose.

iii. Your diabetes team may decide to alter the type of tablet you take to fit in better with your fasting routine.

c) Three daily doses (morning, afternoon and evening). If you are in this group and are taking tablets three times a day then you should first consult your doctor, as the dose and the timings of your tablets will have to be adjusted so that you are able to control your diabetes on twice daily doses. If you are advised to alter your tablets to twice a day then follow the advice from point b), two daily doses.

IT IS VERY IMPORTANT THAT YOU SPEAK TO YOUR DIABETES TEAM FIRST AS ALL TABLETS WORK DIFFERENTLY (some may cause your blood sugar to fall to dangerous levels if not taken properly). Please take note of the advice that your diabetes team gives you. If they are sympathetic to your cause and have advised you not to fast, please take this advice on board and do not fast.

3. INSULIN INJECTIONS AND DIET

a) People with Type 1 Diabetes are often advised not to fast. You can fast if you understand that your insulin regimen will need to be altered.

b) You will need to monitor your blood regularly.

c) Be prepared to break the fast if you have symptoms of low blood sugar (Hypo).

d) You should never stop your insulin.

e) Whether you have Type 1 Diabetes or Type 2 Diabetes, if you are on a basal bolus insulin regimen (e.g. you take background insulin, either once or twice a day and quick acting insulin with meals), you may need to alter your dose of background long acting and alter the timing and amount of quick acting insulin in relation to meals.

f) If you have Type 2 Diabetes and take tablets and night time insulin. You may continue to take your night time insulin, but alter your tablets according to the tablet guidelines mentioned previously.

g) If you are on a pre-mixed insulin regimen e.g. Mixtard 30, Novomix 30, Humulin M3, Humalog mix 25,or mix 50, you may need to seek advice to reduce dose and timings or change to a different insulin regimen during Ramadhān.

4. ADVICE ON DIET

Most health problems are likely to arise from inappropriate diet or as a consequence of over-eating and lack of sleep. There is no need to eat excess food at Iftār or Sahrī. There are two reasons for this:

1) The aim of Ramadhān is to abstain from eating and drinking during sunlight hours. If you then over eat, it can be seen as a reflection of weak discipline.

2) The body adapts to your requirement and will reduce the metabolic rate (the rate at which your body uses energy from food). Most people are less active while fasting. Therefore, if you eat a balanced diet and eat smaller portions of food, it is enough to keep a person healthy and active during the month of Ramadhān.

Contemporary Fiqh   Ramadhān Fast for a Diabetic Person

People with diabetes who decide to fast during Ramadhān need to make sure they:

- Do not skip meals.
- Take all medication as prescribed.
- Avoid over-eating at Sahrī or Iftār as this leads to weight gain and high blood sugar levels.
- Remain as physically active as is normal for them, unless advised otherwise.

The benefits of fasting in Ramadhān appear only in those patients who maintain their diet, avoiding the high calorie and highly processed foods prepared during this time. As fasting may last for as much as 18 hours, the best things to eat are those which release their energy slowly and are rich in fibre. These foods can last for up to 8 hours, while foods which release their energy quickly last for only 3 or 4 hours.

Slow energy release foods include grains and seeds like barley, wheat, oats, millet, semolina, beans, lentils, wholemeal flour, unpolished rice, etc. These are also called complex carbohydrates.

Quick energy release foods generally contain large amounts of sugar or white flour (also known as refined carbohydrates).

Fibre-rich foods include whole wheat, foods containing bran, grains, seeds, vegetables (e.g. green beans, peas, marrow, spinach), fruit with skin, dried fruit (especially dried apricots, figs, and prunes), almonds, etc. It is sensible to:

Contemporary Fiqh   Ramadhān Fast for a Diabetic Person

- If at all possible, have your meal at Sahrī at the proper hour before Subha Sādiq, not at midnight, as this will spread out your energy intake more evenly and result in more balanced blood glucose levels during fasting.
- Drink as much water or sugar-free drinks as possible between Iftār and bedtime and use a sweetener rather than sugar if you need to.
- Fill up on starchy foods such as basmati rice, chapati, or granary bread at Sahrī.
- Include fruits, vegetables, dhal and yoghurt in your meals at Iftār and at Sahrī.
- Limit the amount of sweet foods taken at Iftār.
- Limit your intake of fried and fatty foods (e.g. paratha, puri, samosas, chevera, pakoras, katlamas, fried kebabs, naan or bombay mix) as much as possible.

Common complaints during Ramadhān include:
- Constipation (too little fibre and water in the diet).
- Indigestion (from over-eating, especially of fried, fatty or spicy foods).
- Muscle cramps (not enough vegetables, fruit, meat, or dairy products in the diet).
- Headaches (due to caffeine and tobacco withdrawal).

These minor problems can be easily dealt with by treating the cause. Preparing for Ramadhān by reducing your caffeine intake gradually in the week or so beforehand will help. Smoking is not allowed during Ramadhān, so if you are a smoker, use Ramadhān as an opportunity to give it up – nothing will benefit your general health more! Obviously if you have diabetes you should talk to your diabetes team or ask to see a diabetes specialist Dietician.

It is also important to follow good time management procedures for prayer and other religious activities, sleep, studies, work and physical activities or exercise. A good balance in the amount of time attributed for each activity will lead to a healthier body and mind in Ramadhān.

HYPOGLYCAEMIA LOW BLOOD SUGARS

If the dietary advice and instructions for medications are observed, the chances of sudden changes in blood sugar level are reduced. Even after taking all precautions, a person with diabetes can experience low blood sugar levels (hypos) during the month of Ramadhān. This can be dangerous. The symptoms of low blood sugar levels are hunger, pins and needles, sensations in the lips, weakness, double vision, sweating, drowsiness, trembling, slurring of speech or palpitations (irregular heartbeat). If hypoglycaemia does occur then STOP what you are doing, especially if you are driving or using moving machinery. TAKE two lumps of sugar, OR three glucose tablets, OR two teaspoonful of sugar in squash, OR a glass of water with a couple of biscuits, REPEAT this if the symptoms do not go away within a few minutes. If still not better, call for medical help. If better, TAKE two slices of bread and a cup of milk, or a proper meal, to avoid further 'hypos'. Remember to keep glucose tablets, sugar, or a sugary drink with you at all times in case of emergency.

Do not hesitate to break your fast if you (or others around you) have good reason to believe you are 'going hypo'.

Remember that if you have been advised not to fast by the diabetes team and you had the intention of fasting if you were fit to fast, then Inshā-Allāh, Allāh ﷻ will reward you as if you have fasted! If however, you are no longer able to fast because of your ill health, then it is important that you pay the Fidyah amount that is required of you. The amount of Fidyah is similar to Sadaqatul-Fitr.

Allāh ﷻ Knows Best

Shari'ah Ruling Regarding Three Divorces in One Sitting

By Shaykh Mufti Saiful Islām

Q My wife has received a Fatwa from the Shari'ah Council in Dewsbury that three divorces in one sitting will constitute three divorces. However, a Shari'ah Council in London have said that it will constitute one divorce. Please can you clarify?

A The question being put forward is that if a man gives his wife divorce at least three times in one sitting using clear, explicit words, then does that constitute one divorce or three? Your wife has received a Fatwa from the Shari'ah Council in Dewsbury (Hanafi scholars) who state you are irrevocably divorced. Subsequently, you have received a Fatwa from a Shari'ah Council in London who say only one revocable divorce has taken place. Now, you have asked the Fatwa Department of Jāmiah Khātamun Nabiyyeen to act as an arbitrator in this issue. I apologise for the lengthy reply, however, it is unavoidable when bringing evidence and rejecting the evidence of others.

Background
The Fuqahā state that divorce is of three types:

1. (Ahsan) Best Divorce - To issue divorce whilst the wife is not menstruating and intercourse has not taken place since the last menstruation.

Contemporary Fiqh   Three Divorces in One Sitting

2. (Hasan) Good Divorce - To issue divorce whilst the wife is not menstruating, then to issue a second divorce after the following menstrual cycle and finally, to issue a third divorce after the following menstrual cycle. Hence, three divorces take place in three consecutive pure periods (time in between two menstrual cycles).

3. (Bid'ah) Non-Sunnah Divorce - To issue three divorces in one non-menstruating time or issuing divorce during a menstrual cycle, or to issue divorce whilst the wife is not menstruating but intercourse has taken place since the last menstrual cycle.

(Raddul Muhtār, Vol 4, pg 419-424)

Evidence for the Effect of Three Divorces in One Specific Time

It is narrated from Ikrimah 🙶 that Sayyidunā Abdullāh Ibn Abbās 🙶 said regarding the verse, **"The divorced women should wait three menstrual cycles and it is not permitted for them to conceal that which Allāh has created in their wombs,"** (2:228) "A man who divorces his wife is more entitled to take her back, even if he divorces her three times, then this was abrogated by the verse, **"Divorce is twice..."** (2:229)"
(Abū Dāwūd, Chapter on the abrogation of returning after three divorces, pg 304)

Imām Qurtubi 🙶 states, "The evidence of the majority is very apparent that it is impermissible for a woman who has been divorced three times to return to her first husband until she has had intercourse with another husband and there is no difference lexically or in terms of Shari'ah between issuing them (three divorces) together

Contemporary Fiqh   Three Divorces in One Sitting

or on separate occasions..."(Fathul Bāri, Book on Divorce, Chapter on those who permit three divorces, Vol 9, pg. 456)

It is also known that the Holy Prophet ﷺ would accept the issue of three divorces as valid. Imām Bukhāri ﷺ in his 'al-Jāmius Sahīh' has set a chapter titled, 'The Discussion on the acceptance of three divorces,' which details the episode when Sayyidunā Uwaymir Ajlāni ﷺ accused his wife of adultery in the absence of witnesses (Li'ān – oath of condemnation).

He is reported to have said, "If I take this woman back (after what I have said) I will be called a liar." Therefore, before the Holy Prophet ﷺ issued a verdict, he divorced his wife three times. (Sahīhul Bukhāri, Chapter on the oath of condemnation and whosoever divorces after the oath of condemnation, pg. 799-800; Abū Dāwūd, Chapter on the oath of condemnation, pg. 312)

Imām Abū Dāwūd ﷺ has commented on this Hadīth , "Hence, he issued three divorces in the presence of the Holy Prophet ﷺ, which the Holy Prophet ﷺ declared as valid." (Abū Dāwūd, Chapter on the oath of condemnation, pg 313)

We can summarise the following points from this narration:

1. Three divorces were issued during the era of the Holy Prophet ﷺ.
2. The Holy Prophet ﷺ declared three divorces as valid, even when issued at the same time and when there was no apparent need. The opinion of the four main schools of thought is

| Contemporary Fiqh | Three Divorces in One Sitting |

that after Li'ān there is no need for divorce – the husband and wife are declared separate.

In this very chapter Imām Bukhāri ﷺ quotes another incident; Sayyidah Ā'ishah ﷺ narrates that a man divorced his wife three times. The woman married another man and he divorced her before intercourse had taken place. The Holy Prophet ﷺ was asked, "Is she permissible for the first?" He replied, "No." (Sahīhul Bukhāri, Chapter on those who make three divorces permissible due to the verse of Allāh ﷻ, **"Divorce is twice..."**, pg 791)

We can see from this Hadīth that it was not permissible for her to return after three divorces unless Halālah was performed. One can also see that the Holy Prophet ﷺ did not query whether the divorces were issued together or separately, as the ruling is the same. The following are more episodes highlighting the validity of three divorces, whether issued together or separately:

Saeed Ibn Jubair ﷺ narrates, "I asked Abdullāh Ibn Abbās ﷺ about a man who divorces his wife one thousand times and he replied, 'Three would make his wife illegal for him and with the remainder he is making a mockery of the verses of Allāh ﷻ.'"
(Sunan Dār Qutni, Book of Divorce, Vol 4, pg 10)

Sayyidunā Abdullāh Ibn Umar ﷺ narrates regarding when he divorced his wife, "So I said, 'O Messenger of Allāh ﷺ, if I divorced her three times is it permissible for me that I take her back?' He replied, 'No, she is irrevocably divorced and that would be sinful.'" (Sunan Dāri Qutni, Book on Divorce, Vol 4, pg 20-1)

Contemporary Fiqh   Three Divorces in One Sitting

Evidence For Three Divorces as One Divorce

The Hadīth of Rukānah is presented as an evidence for the occurrence of one divorce, even if three are uttered at one specific time. However, this narration is quoted with different words. In some narrations the words 'divorced three times' are mentioned whilst in others the word al-Battah (absolutely) is mentioned. Imām Abū Dāwūd ﷺ states the one which contains al-Battah is correct. Below is the narration found in the Sunan of Imām Abū Dāwūd ﷺ.

Abdullāh Ibn Ali Ibn Yazīd Ibn Rukānah ﷺ narrates from his father who narrates from his grandfather (i.e. Abdullāh the great-grandson of Rukānah narrates from his father Ali, who in turn narrates from his grandfather, (Rukānah) that he divorced his wife al-Battah, so he went to the Holy Prophet ﷺ who asked him what he intended. Rukānah replied, "One." The Holy Prophet ﷺ asked, "(Do you swear) by Allāh ﷻ?" He replied, "(I swear) by Allāh ﷻ." The Holy Prophet ﷺ said, "Then it is upon what you intended."

Imām Abū Dāwūd ﷺ says this is more correct than the Hadīth of Ibn Juraih, which states that Rukānah divorced his wife three times. This is because Rukānah's family are more knowledgeable of his matters. (Abu Dāwūd, Chapter on al-Battah, pg 307-8)

With this point, the version narrated by Sayyidunā Abdullāh Ibn Abbās ﷺ cannot be taken as evidence.

(Fathul Bāri, Book of Divorce, Vol 9, pg 454)

Therefore, those narrations that quote three divorces are incorrect. The fact that the Holy Prophet ﷺ asked him to swear regarding what he meant provides further evidence. If he said three why would the Holy Prophet ﷺ ask him to swear by Allāh ﷻ that he meant one? Also, this proves that three divorces can take place in one specific time as the word al-Battah has two meanings, three divorces or one divorce and it is determined by the intention of the speaker. Hence, if only one occurred the Holy Prophet ﷺ would not enquire the intention of Rukānah. As three was a possibility he sought clarification.

Next, we will deal with the claim that Sayyidunā Umar Ibn Khattāb's ﷺ Fatwa of three divorces occurring in at one time, is specific to an era/people. Before we delve into the specifics, we need to present some general principles.

- None from the Ulamā-us-Salaf (scholars of the first generation) have stated that this Fatwa was specified to an era, time period or people.

- After the Holy Prophet's ﷺ departure from this world, it is unanimously agreed that nothing can be made permissible or impermissible due to an opinion, whether for a fixed time period or not.

- Those events which took place in the presence of the Holy Prophet ﷺ regarding the validity of three divorces in one sitting, cannot be called novel or innovative when they occurred similarly in the Caliphate of Sayyidunā Umar ﷺ.

| Contemporary Fiqh | Three Divorces in One Sitting |

In fact, this is not the only occasion in which Sayyidunā Umar ؓ re -issued a Fatwa that obtained the consensus of the Sahābah ؓ and Tābi'īn present.

One such incident is the impermissibility of Mut'ah, temporary marriage. Imām Muslim ؒ quotes a Hadīth in which Sayyidunā Jābir Ibn Abdullāh ؓ says, "We used to perform Mut'ah in the era of the Messenger of Allāh ﷺ and Sayyidunā Abū Bakr ؓ until Sayyidunā Umar ؓ forbade it." (Sahīh Muslim, Chapter on Mut'ah)

This is similar in wording to the Hadīth of Sayyidunā Abdullāh Ibn Abbās ؓ, regarding three divorce statements in one sitting. It was considered as one in the era of the Holy Prophet ﷺ, Sayyidunā Abū Bakr ؓ and in the first two/three years of Sayyidunā Umar's ؓ caliphate until he forbade it. The difference is everybody accepts Mut'ah is Harām but they do not accept that three pronouncements in one sitting is equivalent to three.

The question arises that why were people still performing Mut'ah when it was Harām? The answer is simple: at one time Mut'ah was permissible then it was made impermissible. However, all the Companions did not know its abrogation and all Sayyidunā Umar ؓ did was re-issue the original Fatwa and made it known to the masses.

Another evidence put forward to argue that this was a Fatwa of Sayyidunā Umar ؓ, which was his opinion due to his era, is the narration of Abū Sahbā ؓ who asks Sayyidunā Abdullāh Ibn Abbās ؓ about a man who divorces his wife three times in one specific time. Abū Sahbā ﷺ asks, "Were not three taken as one in the time of the Holy Prophet ﷺ and in the time of Sayyidunā Abū Bakr ﷺ, and for three years of the rule of Sayyidunā Umar ﷺ?" He replied, "Yes." (Abū Dāwūd, Chapter on the remainder of the abrogation of return after three divorces, pg 305)

The reason for Sayyidunā Umar's ﷺ statement is that in the golden era, when people divorced, they would mean one divorce and pronounced divorce numerous times for emphasis. As they were from amongst the most upright people who have existed since the dawn of time, they were considered with what they intended. Then in the era of Sayyidunā Umar ﷺ people would pronounce many divorces and claim them as one. That same level of honesty and uprightness no longer remained, as Islām had spread its borders far and wide compared to the era of the Holy Prophet ﷺ and Sayyidunā Abū Bakr ﷺ. So in order to remove the large number of pronouncements and any mockery being made of divorce he stated that the verdict is passed upon what is said. This is the opinion of the Hanafi school of thought in that one cannot claim divorce was uttered three times for emphasis. Rather, judgement would be passed on the number he has pronounced. (Imām Qurtubi and Imām Nawāwi quoted in Fathul Bāri, Book on Divorce, Chapter on those who permit three divorces, Vol 9, pg 456)

Finally, an argument is put forward that three pronouncements should be considered as one because this brings ease to the family. This is not always the case. What if a woman is in a difficult and painful relationship in which she is not provided for and is abused, then one day her husband pronounces three divorces in one specific time. Would she want that to be counted as one or three?

To summarise, according to the Hanafi school of thought, as has been explained in great detail, if a man utters three divorces or more in one specific time, then his wife is irrevocably divorced from him. The woman is free to marry whomsoever she wants. Her Iddah period depends on her circumstances, if she is pregnant then it is until the delivery of the child, if she is pre-menopause then it will be three menstrual cycles and if she is post-menopause it will be three lunar months. If she wants to return to her previous husband, then she has to marry another man and sexual intercourse has to take place before she can be divorced. Following the completion of her Iddah period, she can re-marry her previous husband, so long as she did not intend all this just so she can return to her first husband.

Allāh ﷻ Knows Best

Right of Custody of the Child after Divorce
By Mufti Abdul Waheed

Q Please can you explain in the light of Islām the injunctions pertaining to child custody. Could you clarify the individual roles and responsibilities of parents of physical custody, making decisions on behalf of the child, visitation, contact and stay over, co-operation, upbringing, the mother pursuing work and cultural festivals.

A Children are a great blessing and a trust from Allāh ﷻ. Amongst the rights of the child is that he/she is treated with love and compassion as well as nurtured in a correct way. This can only be attained through a joint responsibility of the mother and father. Compassion and mercy is attained from the mother whilst nurturing and correct upbringing ought to be obtained from the father. Any deficiencies from either side can effect the child, hence, a balance is essential. This is why Islām detests divorce and many times discourages it.

Nevertheless, if for some reason divorce does occur whilst they have children and both demand their right over them, then Islām has also outlined some guidelines and provided the solution to this matter. It should be noted that if both parents have a mutual agreement and compromise between them, then there is no harm as long as no one objects from either side. If however, this is not possible, then the right of custody in Islām will be in the following sequence:

Contemporary Fiqh — Child Custody after Divorce

1. The mother has the first right of custody of the child in Islām.

Sayyidunā Abdullāh Ibn Umar ؓ relates that a woman once came to the Holy Prophet ﷺ and pleaded, "O Messenger of Allāh ﷺ, verily for my son my stomach was his place of refuge, my breast was his water sack (he used to drink milk from) and my lap was for him a place of protection, but his father has divorced me and wishes to snatch him away from me." The Holy Prophet ﷺ said to her, "You have more rights over him as long as you do not marry."

[Abū Dāwūd]

It is understood from the above Hadīth that as long as the mother does not marry (this will be explained later) she has the first right of custody. However, the Fuqahā (Islamic jurists) have stated that this is up to when the child is able to take care of his own bodily functions (i.e. they can eat, drink, bath, clean and dress themselves). For a boy, this has been recognized as when he reaches the age of seven and for a girl, until the age of nine or menstruation.

It is stated in Fatāwa Hindiyya: "The mother and grandmother have the right of custody over the boy until he becomes independent (in terms of taking care of his own bodily functions) and this has been stipulated to the age of seven. Imām Al-Qudūri ؒ states until he eats, drinks and can do Istinjā by himself and for a girl until she menstruates (until the age of nine)."

It is stated in the Mukhtasar of Imām Al-Qudūri that in the case where the mother does not exist (or the right of custody has been taken away from her) then the right of custody will be transferred

45

in the following order:

a) Maternal grandmother to all the way above
b) Paternal grandmother to all the way above
c) Real sister
d) Maternal step sister
e) Paternal step sister
f) Maternal aunt
g) Paternal aunt

2. If after all the aforementioned avenues of females have expired or the child has now become independent in bodily functions (i.e. the boy has reached the age of seven and the girl nine) then the right of custody is transferred to the father. In case the father has died or the right of custody has been taken away from him, then the right of custody will be transferred in the following sequence:

a) Paternal grandfather
b) Paternal uncle
c) Real brother
d) Paternal stepbrother
e) Maternal stepbrother

Notice here, that in the early years of the child's upbringing (regardless of the gender) the mother and the female avenues have been given preference and thereafter, the father and the other male relatives. The wisdom behind this is that in the early years, the child requires love, compassion and motherly care. Thus, the child remains with the mother and the other female relatives, as they are more suitable at this stage. When the boy reaches the age of seven

Contemporary Fiqh	Child Custody after Divorce

and is able to take care of his own bodily necessities, he requires education, financial support and masculine traits.

In the case of the girl, once she reaches the age of nine or menstruates, then she is in need of education, protection and financial support, in which case the father now is responsible for, which is why the custody is then transferred to him.

Nevertheless, the boy remains in the custody of the father until puberty at which point he is able to take care of himself and is mature and wise enough to understand. Thereafter, he is free to choose with whom he stays, either with the mother, the father or by himself. As for the girl, the father's custody remains until she is married as this is the father's responsibility, or she reaches the age of understanding and becomes mature enough to deal with her basic essentials on her own. [Durrul Mukhtār]

3. The right of custody is revoked if:

a) The mother marries a non-Mahram man to the child (i.e. someone from outside the family etc.) by which the child will be affected. (the Hadīth mentioned previously)

b) Either of them apostates (may Allāh ﷻ forbid).

c) The woman seeks remuneration for the upbringing of the child whereas there is another female relative willing to raise the child free of charge.

d) Either of them is indulged in open sin that will affect the child.

e) The woman cannot attend to the child's attention due to her leaving the house very frequently whereby the child will be affected.

Contemporary Fiqh   Child Custody after Divorce

4. In either case, whether the child is in the custody of the mother or the father, the financial responsibility lies on the father's shoulder (Hidāyah). To the extent that when the mother has the right of custody but does not have a shelter, then the father must also provide that. [Durrul Mukhtār]

As long as the father financially provides for the child whilst he/she is in the custody of the mother, then there is no need for her to work. If however, there is a genuine need for the mother to work and the child is affected by this, then as mentioned before, the right of custody will be transferred to someone else in the order aforementioned, otherwise not.

5. As far as making decisions on the child's behalf is concerned, then generally speaking, only that person, in whose custody the child is in can determine this, as long as that decision does not infringe the laws of Islām. For instance, the mother cannot prevent the father visiting the child and like-wise vice-versa.

6. With regards to contact and visitation, then both parent have the rights regardless of whose custody the child is in. It is stated in Fatāwa Hindiyyah (a famous encyclopedia of the Hanafi Fiqh): "If the child is with one parent then he/she cannot prevent the other from seeing (or visiting) him."

The Islamic Law has not stipulated precisely how often the parents can visit the child. However, this can be mutually agreed by both parties. Visitation does not restrict to merely seeing the child but also entails talking to him, seeking information (e.g. medical records etc). As far as staying over is concerned, then this can also be mutually agreed between both parties. However, it is a great sin to prevent either of the parents from visiting or speaking to the child. Unfortunately, nowadays some parents use the child as a weapon to deprive either the mother or the father from visiting. This is absolutely wrong and a major sin because this eventually leads to hatred and conflict between both parties.

7. Cultural and family festivals generally have no connection with the child's custody. Every scenario is judged individually. What should be remembered here is that the festival should not consist of any un-Islamic traditions that are acts of sin within themselves.

Allāh ﷻ Knows Best

Woman Exercising in her Home
Dr Rafaqat Rashid

Q I am a mother of 5 children, Alhamdulillāh. However, I have very little opportunity to exercise as I do not leave the house very much. Do you have any tips on exercises I could do in the house to keep my weight down?

A There are many ways to keep fit just in the house. My advise would be for you to spare at least 30 minutes of your time performing moderate exercise each day to keep fit and healthy. Safe exercising is an essential, which means you warm up before exercise. One method to warm up would be to stretch the muscles gently (warm up exercises-leaflets and info are easily available from most health shops or the gym). Jogging on the spot for 5 minutes is one good method.

Some Tips for Exercising at Home:
- Climbing stairs as circuits, up and down the stairs with speed would be one circuit. Gradually increase this in number from 7 circuits upwards. Alternatively, you could use one of the stairs as a step-up. This will strengthen your leg muscles and is good for the heart.
- If you have children in the house, supervising them can sometimes be an issue and prevent you from certain exercises. Remember, playing with children is a work out itself.
- Running around the house (when safe), preferably in the garden or playing hide and seek can contribute to the 30 minutes a day exercise.

| Contemporary Fiqh | Women Exercising at Home |

- Following exercise DVDs or videos is not permissible in Islām if it involves listening to music and performing dance routines as part of the aerobic exercise. Some suggestions are to get pamphlets and books on aerobic exercises not involving dancing, do Dhikr as you are exercising so as to gain reward at the same time or listen to tapes/CD's of Islamic lectures, nashīds etc.
- Purchase basic exercise equipment. I would not recommend expensive large equipment but rather, one simple piece of equipment such as an exercise ball, bike or treadmill. The aim is not to convert the house into a gym.
- If using weights is not your style, then using the floor is sufficient for sit-ups, leg raises, press-ups etc.
- Finally, doing the housework is an excellent way to exercise and it cleans up the house at the same time!

The list below gives you an idea of approximately how many calories you can burn in an hour of housework:

- Ironing: 120
- Grocery Shopping: 175
- Making beds: 135
- Mopping/sweeping: 220
- Painting: 135
- Scrubbing floors: 400
- Shelving groceries: 220
- Vacuuming: 175
- Washing Dishes: 120
- Washing windows: 250

Treatment for Hair Loss
Dr Rafaqat Rashid

Q I have suffered with small bald patches on my scalp for the past few years which have been quite unsightly. I have been told that this condition is called Alopecia and that there is no cure. Please can you advise me of any treatments you may know of or any tips? I am a 23 year old woman and this has really stressed me out.

A I really do sympathise. It cannot be easy having such a condition at such a young age and I believe it is much more difficult if you are female. If what you have is truly Alopecia, then more than likely it is 'Alopecia Areata'. Alopecia means hair loss. This is a condition that affects approximately 2% of the population. Males and females are equally affected and this usually occurs in the younger age groups.

This condition usually presents suddenly as small bald patches in the scalp which follow a number of different patterns. They can sometimes re-grow, disappear completely or become larger or smaller, the pattern is very variable in different individuals. They can also affect eyebrows, beards and the moustache area in men.

25% of those affected have a close relative with a similar condition (i.e. it can be inherited) and the cause of the condition is not truly known though the process is auto-immune (the body mistakes the hair follicles as foreign and as a result, there are increased white cells around the follicles preventing hair growth in that area). If the

Contemporary Fiqh | Treatment for Hair Loss

immune reaction goes the hair begins to grow again. Options of treatment are as follows: If there are 2 or less bald patches, the doctor will normally tell you that it is likely to grow again and there is no need for further treatment. This usually can take more than 3 months. One should have patience at this stage. It is reassuring to know that it does not harm the general health of a person and is likely to disappear with time.

Other medical options are as follows:

- **Steroid Injections** - This involves injecting the affected area and is only suitable for small patches. It usually needs to be done repeatedly, every couple of weeks, a few times, by a skin specialist.

- **Steroid Cream or Gel etc.** - This is not as effective as the injection but can be tried on patches which are too big for injections. However, this is not always successful.

- **Minoxidil Solution** - This again, is not as effective as the above but sometimes can be worth a try and is an option for those who have many big patches.

- **Topical Immunotherapy** - This is for bigger, widespread patches but needs to be done by a specialist, though not all specialists carry out this procedure. It is more effective than the other procedures. It usually means a substance is placed on the affected area and it requires regular application over a long period of a few months at least.

| Contemporary Fiqh | Treatment for Hair Loss |

- **Dithranol** - Not as commonly used because it is quite messy and is less effective than topical immunotherapy. It is used on larger areas for many weeks and can cause local irritation also.

- **Other Therapies** - These are not commonly used but can include light therapy (PUVA) and immunosuppressant medication (i.e. cyclosporin).

- **Complementary Therapy** - Such as herbal, acupuncture or aromatherapy.

- **Wigs -** It is generally not permissible in Islām for men to wear wigs though there may be exceptions for some women. The issue would have to be discussed with a Mufti for individual cases.

These are some of the treatments that are usually tried and you would have to discuss these options with your doctor. May Allāh ﷻ make it easy for you and cure you of this illness. Āmīn.

Allāh ﷻ Knows Best

Women & Nutrition
Dr Rafaqat Rashid

Q I have been prescribed Calceos (vitamin D supplements) by my doctor because I have a deficiency and I was told that this is because I wear a Niqāb. Is this true? Can you advise me on this?

A Vitamin D deficiency means that there is not enough vitamin D in the body and this vitamin is vital for strong bones and muscles. Vitamin D is produced under the skin with exposure to sunlight. The UV light from the sun helps to produce this vitamin and thus, those of us who have dark skin need more sun. Vitamin D is also found in certain foods: liver, some fish (mainly oily fish such as herring, sardines, pilchards, trout, salmon, tuna and mackerel), egg yolk, and 'fortified' foods (which have vitamin D added) such as some margarines and breakfast cereals.

Vitamin D deficiency is more likely to develop in the following risk people:

- **Pregnant or breastfeeding women** - The baby needs vitamin D for muscle and bone growth.

- **Breastfed babies whose mothers lack vitamin D** - Continue breastfeeding but also give baby multivitamin drops (e.g. Dalivit, Abidec).

- **Those who have little skin exposure to the sun** - Refers to mainly those people who may wear Niqāb/Hijāb and have

Contemporary Fiqh   Women and Nutrition

little exposure to the sun. It would therefore be advisable for these women to sit out in front of the sun around the house or garden where there is privacy on a regular basis (approximately 15-30 minutes 3 times a week depending on the darkness of the skin) and more in the winter. In addition, they should eat a healthy diet, rich in vitamin D.

- **Medical conditions that affect vitamin D metabolism** - These include conditions such as coeliac disease, crohns disease and some liver and kidney diseases etc.

- **Certain medication** - These medications can also affect the metabolism of vitamin D (e.g. carbamezepine, phenytoin etc.)

- **People with dark skin** - Dark skin prevents full absorption of the sun light as a result of increased melanin in the skin which actually protects against sunlight.

- **Those with a family history of Vitamin D deficiency or poor diet.**

A few points to note are that vitamin D deficiency is quite common, approximately 2 in 10 adults in the UK have it and 9 out of 10 South Asian adults have it. Most of these adults do not complain of any symptoms and thus do not know they have this deficiency. The symptoms in adults are usually muscle and bone pain and in children bow legs if severe enough. Vitamin D deficiency has not been proven to cause serious conditions other than symptoms of pain in some patients. However, if it becomes very severe, it can

Contemporary Fiqh | Women and Nutrition

cause softening and weakness of the bones in both adults and children. The treatment is as simple as taking Vitamin D supplements in chewable tablet form or liquid, or in more serious conditions taking a vitamin D injection.

Q **Dear Doctor Sāhib, I am pregnant at the moment and would like you to advise me on any vitamins I should take and what I should avoid. Also, can you explain whether intercourse with my husband can be harmful to me or my baby?**

A Pregnancy is an important period for a mother, as the mother has to "eat for two" and thus she needs to be cautious about what she eats and drinks. There are certain vitamins that are not harmful to a normal adult but can be potentially harmful to the baby during pregnancy and there are those nutrients that are recommended in pregnancy.

A good balanced diet will give you all the vitamins and minerals you need, though taking the following vitamins as supplements is advised as follows:

- **Folic Acid** - During the first three months of pregnancy (and preferably before becoming pregnant) a woman should take folic acid as it is important during pregnancy for the development of the baby's nervous system. This is usually prescribed by the GP.

- **Iron** - During pregnancy, a woman's body needs more iron than usual to produce all the blood needed to supply nutrition to the placenta. Usually, a blood test is taken and if the patient is anaemic, iron supplements are given by the GP. Good sources of iron are green vegetables, such as broccoli, spinach, strawberries, muesli and wholemeal bread.

The following vitamins should only be taken under the advice of a medical professional. These are highlighted below:

- **Vitamin A** - A balanced diet will normally give you all the vitamin A you need. Too much vitamin A can harm the baby. For this reason it is best to avoid liver or liver products and fish oil supplements (e.g. cod liver oil).

- **Vitamin B12** - A good intake of this vitamin is important as it helps to make new cells and build the nervous system of the baby. Unless one has a vegan diet, there is usually sufficient amounts of this vitamin in a standard balanced diet containing meat, fish, eggs, milk, hard cheese and fortified breakfast cereals.

- **Vitamin C** - There has been some talk about vitamin C being potentially harmful in very high doses. However, eating fresh oranges or drinking fresh orange juice is a good way of taking a safe amount of Vitamin C in your diet and will also help with constipation that can affect many women in pregnancy.

- **Vitamin D** - Calcium and Vitamin D usually go hand in hand and are quite important in the diet as they help the development of the baby's bones and teeth. One should talk to a medical professional if there is a need to take this. I believe that all Muslim women who wear Hijāb or Niqāb should take this as a supplement during pregnancy as they usually have less skin exposure to the sun and this vitamin is produced under the skin with sun exposure. You are advised to talk to your GP or midwife.

My final advice regarding this subject is that, it is not advisable to take supplements randomly without medical advice, especially in large quantities. This is because some vitamins could in fact cause harm to your baby, rather than help their growth.

To answer the second part of your question regarding intercourse in pregnancy. You can continue as far into pregnancy, right up until birth, as long as you and your husband are comfortable. There are a few reasons why you should not have intercourse during certain periods during pregnancy. These include vaginal bleeding, infection or preterm labour.

Allāh ﷻ Knows Best

Becoming a Female Doctor - What are My Limitations?

Dr Rafaqat Rashid

Q I am a recently graduated female doctor, applying for a residency (post-graduate degree). I have the option of applying for about 20 different subjects like Internal Medicine, Obstetrics and Gynecology, Pediatrics, Surgery, Anesthesia, Radiology, Emergency Medicine and Psychiatry, among others. I need to know if there is anything impermissible about females treating male patients, from a purely Islamic point of view. Many people have told me again and again, it is alright, and they give the reason that we need good Muslim female doctors, whether physicians, or surgeons or obstetricians (maternity doctors) because the female patients need them. However, in these years of residency training, we end up having to examine both female and male patients, and quite extensively, in surgical cases. I know we need female surgeons as well, because breast patients find it extremely embarrassing to go to a male surgeon. However, that does not justify anything by itself. I am looking for a valid point from a reliable source.

A There are two issues of concern here:

1. Awra - (exposing parts of the body which are not permissible to a non-Mahram)

2. Khalwa - (seclusion with a non-mahram)

Both of the above are not permitted in Islām. However, exceptions are made in cases such as medical need or necessity. Most of the Fuqahā agree upon this but with the following conditions:

1. Real need (necessity permits the impermissible)
There must be a real need. Real need would fall within the scope that examination of a certain anatomy of a person is required to ascertain information that is likely to:

- **Support a diagnosis or therapy** - This can include a broad system examination for cancer, surgical treatment or a process of investigation (e.g. transvaginal U/S).

- **Prevent medical liability** - As this would be threatening to one's career and would be a requirement by the medical regulatory bodies and medical law.

- **For educational reasons** - i.e. learning how to examine a system or taking an exam.

Note: One must bear in mind if any of the above can be avoided without medico-legal risk then this would be a better option. For example:- If it is obvious that there is a small uncomplicated boil around the groin from the history of the patient and there is no evidence of red flags, then it would be better just to provide antibiotics rather than examine the groin etc.

2. Availability of appropriate gender health professional
If the patient is of opposite gender, then all effort must be made to

refer the patient to a health professional who is of the same gender as the patient. This will depend on availability. Ideally for a Muslim female patient the order of preference is a Muslim female, a non-Muslim female, a practicing Muslim male and finally a non-Muslim male.

For a Muslim male patient a Muslim male, then a non-Muslim male, a Muslim female and finally a non-Muslim female. Non-availability will only be justified with the following reasons:

- The other health professional is not willing to see or examine the patient.
- There is no available health professional who fulfils the required experience or skill level. (e.g. a male consultant gynaecologist would be considered permissible even if a female Muslim gynaecologist is available but does not have the required expertise).
- There is no obligation to undergo hardship in seeking an appropriate gender health professional of sufficient expertise to the extent that it could be detrimental to ones career. For instance, if patients have been placed on ones named clinic list, it would be considered serious hardship to see only the same gender patients, even if an appropriate gender health professional is available as this could be detrimental to ones career and reputation. The principle of 'hardship begets facility' will apply.
- If there is an emergency and the first health professional available is not of the same gender - the principle 'A greater harm is eliminated by [tolerating] a lesser harm' will apply.

Note: Circumstances where there is a need to examine the genital/

anal areas of males and females, or breasts of females would require one to exert some element of hardship in seeking a health professional of appropriate gender, as these are considered areas of Shahwa (sexual organs or areas of modesty) even to health professionals. It is therefore discouraged for males to specialise in areas of obstetrics and gynaecology or females to specialise in urology where the focus of that speciality are those systems.

3. Not to exceed limits of Khalwa and exposure of Awra - (harm is to be eliminated within reasonable limits)

Awra:
- If any part of the Awra must be uncovered, then all effort must be made to expose only the minimum required and to cover it as soon as possible.
- If any part of the anatomy is to be touched, then one must ensure that the minimum of touching is done to ascertain what is required and for the least reasonable period.

Khalwa:
- The ethical and legal right of privacy competes with the obligation of Khalwa. This is because there may be times where one needs to see a patient alone so as not to breach confidentiality of an embarrassing medical issue, even before the husband or wife. For this reason, because of medico-legal requirements, a medical professional would not be liable under Islamic Law if he/she consulted with the opposite gender alone with the same conditions as "Availability of appropriate gender health professional" above.

- When discussing about, or examining the areas of Shahwa one should make every effort to do this in the company of the patient's spouse. This should be done to the extent that the above point allows. Examining patients Awra in direct view of the patients Mahram, other than the spouse, is not permissible if this is considered Awra for the Mahram also. If the patient insists on this then there is no Shari' liability on the health professional.
- Examining the areas of Shahwa should only be done in direct view of a chaperone of the same gender as the patient. For example, when a female doctor is obligated to examine a male patient, a male chaperone is advised if possible (this situation should be avoided by all reasonable means).

Final Note: One must always uphold professionalism (Ādāb) in ones conduct. This is a requirement in both Islamic Law as well as a medico-legal obligations.

[I have not inserted evidential text. However, reference should be made to Imām Ibn Ābidīn 🙵, Raddul Muhtār, Al-Qawā'id Al-Fiqhiyya of Dharar and Dharūrah (harm and necessity), Al-Ashbāh Wan-Nadhā'ir of Ibn Nujaym 🙵 and of Imām Suyūti 🙵.]

Allāh 🙵 Knows Best

Hijāb From Non-Mahram In-Laws

By Mufti Abdul Waheed

Q What is the Islamic ruling regarding maintaining Hijāb (veiling) with brother-in-laws?

A Your situation is not only restricted to the Niqāb itself, but also to other aspects of Hijāb. I say this because unfortunately, many people today become strict adherents to the covering of the face, yet overlook the other aspects of Hijāb. Hijāb is a broad area which entails many other aspects of modesty such as the controlling of the mind, the tongue, one's conduct towards others etc. As Muslims, we must follow Islām in its entirety and not partially.

Furthermore, to make claims such as, 'Niqāb has nothing to do with Islām' is wrong. Such remarks are on account of ignorance and the lack of understanding of Dīn in its true sense. There are many evidences in the Holy Qur'ān and Hadīth that necessitate the covering of the face for a woman from non-Mahram men which will be presented later on in this article.

Moreover, many people often overlook the injunctions of observing Hijāb with non-Mahram relatives, such as brother in-laws, with the assumption that they are similar to blood relatives. The reality is, that their rulings are dissimilar from one another. It is compulsory to observe the rules of Hijāb towards non-Mahram relatives such as brother in-laws and sister in-laws and the immediate and extended family members from either side.

Contemporary Fiqh   Hijāb From Non-Mahram In-Laws

To observe Hijāb with non-Mahram in-laws is established from the following Hadīth:

Sayyidunā Uqba Ibn Āmir ﷺ relates that the Holy Prophet ﷺ warned, "Beware of entering upon women." A man of the Ansār asked, "O Messenger of Allāh ﷺ, what about in-laws?" He replied, "In-laws are death." (Bukhāri, Muslim)

In this text the Arabic term 'Hamw' is used which refers to brother in-laws. This demonstrates the severity of not maintaining the rules of Hijāb with ones non-Mahram in-laws (e.g. informal interaction with them and to remain secluded with them unnecessarily) which can possibly lead to further mischief if ignored. As previously mentioned, Hijāb entails many other aspects in addition to covering the face. I will primarily outline below some other aspects pertaining to 'The Rules of Hijāb' which are relevant to your situation:

1) To conceal the Awrah (private parts)

The Awrah of a man begins below the navel extending below the knees whereas, the Awrah of a woman in the presence of a non-Mahram (including in-laws), is her entire body apart from her face, hands up to the wrist and feet from just below the ankles.

2) The prohibition of Khalwah (seclusion) with a non-Mahram

The classical scholars of Islām define Khalwa as to remain secluded with a non-Mahram person, without the presence of a third person (Mahram) and a third person cannot gain access or finds it difficult

Contemporary Fiqh | Hijāb From Non-Mahram In-Laws

to enter upon them, whilst they are secluded with one another. This kind of seclusion is categorically forbidden in the following Hadīth:

Sayyidunā Abdullāh Ibn Abbās ﷺ relates that the Holy Prophet ﷺ said, "No man should remain secluded with any woman (that is marriageable to him) and a woman should not travel except a Mahram accompanies her." (Bukhāri, Muslim)

3) Informal interaction with the opposite gender

It is not permissible to freely interact with the opposite gender nor have a casual relationship in their tone of voice and conduct. Allāh ﷻ states in the Holy Qur'ān, **"Be not soft in your speech lest he in whose heart is a disease should be inclined (with lustful desire) but rather speak in an honourable manner."** (33:32)

"And when you ask them for anything then ask them from behind the screen; this is purer for your hearts and their hearts." (33:53)

Although the above two verses are addressing the noble wives of the Holy Prophet ﷺ, they are applicable to every Muslim woman because their noble lifestyles serve as an exemplary role model for our Muslim sisters today. The reason for this injunction is to protect the modesty of the society and to prevent Fitna (mischief) to infiltrate within the Muslim community.

4) Lowering the gaze

Allāh ﷻ states, **"Say to the believing men to lower their gazes and protect their private parts; this is purer for them. Verily, Allāh is well aware of what you do. And say to the believing women to lower their gaze and guard their private parts and manifest not their adornment except that which is apparent."** (24:30-31)

The gaze must be lowered as much as possible and one must not look at the opposite gender unnecessarily.

5) To apply perfume and wear high heels that attract the opposite gender

A woman must ensure that she must not apply excessive fragrance or walk in high heels that will attract the opposite non-Mahram gender.

Allāh ﷻ states in the Holy Qur'ān, **"And let them not stamp their feet in order to reveal that which they conceal of their adornment."** (24:31)

Sayyidunā Abū Mūsā ؓ narrates that the Holy Prophet ﷺ said, "If a woman applies perfume and passes by a group of (non-Mahram) men, and they smell her perfume, she is such and such." The narrator says that the Holy Prophet ﷺ used stern words. (Abū Dāwūd)

6) Niqāb (covering the face)

There are evidences suggesting the covering of the face to be necessary. Allāh ﷻ states in the Holy Qur'ān, **"O Prophet! Instruct your wives, your daughters and the believing women to draw their cloaks (Jilbābs) over them."** (33:59)

a) According to Sayyidunā Abdullāh Ibn Abbās ؓ, Jilbāb refers to that cloak which conceals the entire body of a woman. Many classical scholars who were masters in the commentaries of the Holy Qur'ān, such as Ibn Jarīr at-Tabari ؒ, interpret the meaning of Jilbāb to refer to that cloak which covers the entire body of a woman apart from the eyes to see with, some say to leave one eye uncovered. (Rūhul Ma'āni)

b) Sayyidunā Qais Ibn Shammās ؓ relates that a woman came to the Holy Prophet ﷺ who was known as Umme Khallād and she had a Niqāb over her face. She came to enquire regarding her son who was killed. One Companion said to her, "You are enquiring regarding your murdered son whilst you wear a Niqāb?" She replied, "Distress has befallen on my son but not on my modesty." (Abū Dāwūd)

c) Sayyidah Ā'ishah ؓ relates, "We were with the Holy Prophet ﷺ whilst in Ihrām and many people would pass by us whilst riding their animals. When they would come close, we would draw a cloak to cover our faces and once they had passed by us, then we would uncover our faces." (Abū Dāwūd)

The above evidences are sufficient in suggesting that the covering of the face is part of the Islamic teachings and a fundamental requirement for our women to practice, for safeguarding their modesty. There are also more evidences from the Ahādīth. Based on the above mentioned evidences, the classical jurists from the Hanafi school of thought have ruled that the covering of the face for women is Wājib even though the face is not part of the Satr. This is due to the ample amount of evidences regarding it from the Holy Qur'ān and Sunnah and also because of the prevalent corruption in our society.

Having said this, an important point I would like to address is that Islām also provides solutions and flexibility in circumstances of prevalent difficulty and hardship. In those situations where a person has to undergo severe hardship and difficulty, or a genuine need arises then, due to such unavoidable circumstances, certain aspects of Islamic commands are uplifted and relaxed depending upon the level of difficulty. However, this only applies to that extent which is necessary. Such genuine needs are referred to as Hājah.

Although it is necessary to cover the face, there are exceptional cases where this command is uplifted for example, giving testimony in an Islamic court where a judge must see the face of the witness, extreme congestion or any other circumstantial and genuine need. (Takmila Fathul Mulhim)

For a woman living in the same house where there is frequent interaction with non-Mahram relatives, such as brother in-laws, or

Contemporary Fiqh | Hijāb From Non-Mahram In-Laws

there is frequent visitation if they live separately, wearing the Niqāb can sometimes become burdensome. Therefore, the scholars have given the following concessions in regards to the Niqāb:

1) Rather than wearing a Niqāb, she may wear a Shawl or a scarf over her head and merely place the end of her scarf or shawl to cover her face in the presence of her brother in-law.

2) Shaykh Abdur Rauf Sakharvi, a senior Mufti of Dārul-Ulūm in Karachi, states that in such scenarios a woman may leave her face uncovered as long as her Awrah in the presence of a non-Mahram remains covered at all times.

It should be remembered that this concession is restricted to the covering of the face only. The remaining five aspects of Hijāb such as the covering of the Awrah, avoiding total seclusion with a non-Mahram, informal interaction and conversation, refraining from applying fragrance and lowering the gaze as much as possible cannot be compromised. Apart from the concession given to uncover the face, the other aspects of Hijāb must be strictly adhered to. Violating any of them would be an act of sin.

In spite of the concession given to uncovering the face, if a woman still wishes to conceal her face in front of her brother in-laws, then that would be her act of discretion and piety. No family member and neither her husband can compel her to act contrary to it.

Nevertheless, a woman must ensure that the covering of the face in such difficult situations should not lead to great hostility and animosity between the family members. One must realise that such situations must be handled with care and wisdom rather than having a strict approach because this could also aggravate family problems. If such consequences are inevitable, then it would be advisable to act upon the concession in order to avert the hostility rather than acting upon ones own piety and then create family problems. However, as mentioned earlier, the other aspects of Hijāb must be strictly followed by both men and women. Additionally, in covering the face, the woman must also see how long she can maintain it because often in the initial stages, an individual would become stringent in acting upon piety, yet she is not able to maintain it for a longer period due to pressure. Likewise, in your situation, by observing the Niqāb, you need to see whether you are able to maintain it throughout your life or not. If not then you are better off acting upon the concession.

In conclusion, the rules of Hijāb entail other aspects of concealment as well as covering the face. Niqāb is not a traditional practice as some have assumed. Rather, it is a religious duty established from the Holy Qur'ān and Sunnah. However, in the case where there is frequent interaction between brother-in-laws, the laws of covering the face can be relaxed, especially if it will intensify family problems provided that the remaining rules of Hijāb are not compromised.

Allāh ﷻ Knows Best

Contemporary Fiqh | Organ Transplantation

Organ Transplant and Blood Transfusion
By Mufti Abdul Waheed

Q I would be very appreciative if you could shed some light on the following questions:

1. What is the Islamic ruling regarding blood transfusion?
2. Are organ transplant permissible?
3. Is it permissible to use artificial limbs?
4. Is it permissible to donate an organ to someone who is in urgent need of it during his life or to make a will to donate?

A Before I begin to answer the above mentioned questions in detail, I would like to primarily discuss certain principles which are relevant to all of the aforementioned questions. This will hopefully, by the will of Allāh ﷻ, enable us to facilitate the understanding of the above mentioned issues. Mufti Shafī Sāhib ﷺ in his book on organ transplants has discussed certain principles before elaborating on the issue of organ transplant. In summary, these are as follows:

1. All Those Factors Prohibited for Human Beings are Harmful
All those things and factors that Allāh ﷻ has prohibited are detrimental for mankind at large. Allāh ﷻ is the Creator of the universe and the Creator of every living thing. It is our firm belief that He is the Benefactor and our Creator, so He himself knows in His Divine Wisdom what is beneficial for us and what is harmful for us.

He has laid down all the instructions in the Holy Qur'ān of the

Contemporary Fiqh   Organ Transplantation

do's and don'ts in His Divine Wisdom and sent the Holy Prophet ﷺ to explain and clarify His Commandments. For instance, Allāh ﷻ has forbidden theft and robbery. Although there may be some benefits therein but this crime has more harmful effects compared to its benefits. There are certain prohibitions, for instance consuming a dead body where a layman as well as a doctor will know that such consumption is extremely detrimental for the physical body. However, there are other prohibitions that may not be harmful to the body but they are harmful to the soul. Therefore, Allāh ﷻ has prohibited them. Allāh ﷻ Himself knows better because He is the All Knower whereas mankind is unable to detect anything which causes harm to the soul. A human being's intellect and knowledge is very limited in comparison to Allāh's ﷻ Knowledge.

In summary, whatever Allāh ﷻ has forbidden for mankind, He has done so for our benefit and for our success.

2. The Dignity of a Human Being

Allāh ﷻ has created mankind in the best form and honoured mankind above all of His other creations throughout the heavens and the earth. In the physical form, mankind is esteemed as Allāh ﷻ states; **"Indeed We have created mankind in the best of form"** (95:4). In terms of knowledge mankind has been honoured; **"He taught mankind of what he knew not"** (96:5). Likewise, He has conferred mankind above all of His creations; **And verily We have honoured the children of Ādam (17:70).**

Allāh ﷻ has made the animals subservient to human beings whereby much benefits can be derived from them in the right way

Contemporary Fiqh   Organ Transplantation

for instance, their milk, meat, skin etc. Similarly, at times of extreme difficulties where there is certainty of loss of life or for medication purposes certain things are permitted to save ones life or to prevent the health from deteriorating.

3. No Human Being is the Owner of their Own Body

It is our firm belief that everything that Allāh ﷻ has created belongs to Him. Every organ in our body belongs to Allāh ﷻ as He himself states in the Holy Qurān; **"To Him belongs all that which is in the heavens and all that is in the earth and all that is between them and all that is under the soil" (20:6).** Therefore, it is not permitted for any human being to utilise any organ however and whichever way he/she wishes. This is why Allāh ﷻ has sent down instructions for us to follow. However, in spite the fact that everything belongs to Allāh ﷻ, Allāh ﷻ has entrusted us with this body to test whether we employ it in the right or the wrong way and we will receive our final recompense in the Hereafter.

4. Some Flexibilities in Islām Regarding Medical Treatment

In spite the fact that this body of ours belongs to Allāh ﷻ, He has entrusted it to us and has honoured it. For this reason it is imperative to employ this body in the manner that Allāh ﷻ and His Messenger ﷺ has instructed us and to look after it well. It is a grave sin to neglect the body when it requires any medical treatment as this body has a right over oneself and Muslims are instructed to seek medical treatment when the body demands it.

The Holy Prophet ﷺ said; "O' servants of Allāh ﷻ seek medical treatment, for verily Allāh ﷻ has not placed any illness except

Contemporary Fiqh

Organ Transplantation

along with it He has placed a cure for it apart from one illness that is old age (Ahmad, Tirmizi and Abū Dāwūd).

As we see nowadays, new illnesses have emerged which were unheard of in the past, yet Allāh ﷻ through His infinite mercy has created cures for them. Every era doctors and those specialized in the fields of medicine discover and form new medicines which are able to cure new illnesses. Thus, in terms of medical treatment Islām is somewhat flexible, considering the state of necessity, and has permitted the consumption of unlawful substance if such substance will guarantee cure and its effectiveness is certain. In the state of IDHTIRĀR (where there is certainty of loss of life) consuming unlawful animals is permissible where no lawful animal is available to save ones life and to benefit from only that amount with which a person's hunger can be satisfied without exceeding the boundaries. Similar principle will apply in seeking medical treatment, that only to that extent of which is required is permitted.

5. A detailed explanation of Idhtirār and the definition of Hājat and Manfa'at etc.

This principle will elaborate on the meaning of the term Idhtirār used in the Holy Qur'ān and its implication because unfortunately many people have misunderstood its application. The Arabic word Dharūrat is derived from Idhtirār which has a different implication from that which is used in Urdu. The term Hājat is also different from that of Idhtirār. Shaykh Hamawy ﷺ in his collection on the commentary of Al-Ashbāh wan-Nadhā'ir states that there are five categories which are as follows:

Dharūrat or Idhtirār: This is defined as a person who is in a situation where by not using an unlawful substance or thing, there is certainty of loss of life which results in a person to be on the point of death. In such extreme circumstances, it would be permissible to use unlawful substances. All the scholars unanimously agree to this.

Hājat: This means that by not utilising an unlawful substance or thing there is no apprehension of the loss of life but the fear of health extremely deteriorating is present, resulting in one not being able to conduct his/her daily duties properly. There are differences of opinions amongst the jurists of whether or not it is permissible to use unlawful things or not.

Manfa'at (Benefit): By utilising something it gives strength to the body or gives other additional benefits. But by not using it, ones body is not harmed and neither is ones life in jeopardy. In these circumstances, unlawful things never become permissible for one to use and in doing so he/she will be held responsible for it on the Day of Judgement.

Zīnat (Adornment): Using it does not result in physical strength but it merely adorns the body. Likewise, prohibited things used in this way do not become permissible.

Fudhūl (Extravagance): This is a step beyond the fourth category which is not permissible at all.

The categories which are up for discussion are the first two. The

Contemporary Fiqh · Organ Transplantation

major difference between Dharūrat and Hājat is that in the case of Dharūrat one's life is in jeopardy resulting in one being at the point of death whereas in the state of Hājat one's life is not in danger.

The term Idhtirār mentioned in the Holy Qur'ān usually refers to the aforementioned meaning and almost all of the commentators have agreed to this. Many factors will be taken into consideration and for a scholar to give the correct verdict he must analyse the whole scenario (i.e. how serious it is, how much certainty is there, are there any other alternatives or any other solutions etc).

An example for this could be, that if someone is compelled to renounce their faith to become an apostate, and the perpetrator has pointed a gun at the victim and threatened to kill him if he does not comply, then by merely having a gun being pointed at the victim will not be considered Mudhtar in the terminology of Shari'ah. The whole scenario will be taken into account. If the victim is one hundred percent certain that the perpetrator is serious and he has no other means to resort to defend himself, or he is surrounded by many of them and furthermore, he is certain about the loss of his life, then in such extreme circumstances it would be permitted for the victim to renounce his faith verbally as long as his heart is content with faith.

This was the case with Sayyidunā Ammār Ibn Yāsir ﷺ when the Pagans of Makkah persecuted him endlessly and exerted pressure upon him to renounce his faith. Sayyidunā Ammār ﷺ verbally renounced his faith but his heart was content with Imān and Allāh ﷻ and His Messenger ﷺ had excused him. Sayyidunā Ammār ؓ had no other means to defend himself and was certain that his life was in jeopardy. Similarly, this will be applicable in this context.

On the other hand, if the victim is certain that the perpetrator will not pull the trigger, but has merely pointed the gun to intimidate him or the victim is able to resort to other means to defend himself then he will not be classified as Mudhtar. Thus, it would not be permissible to renounce his faith verbally.

Correspondingly, it is inadequate for an ill person to merely have the apprehension of the loss of life for unlawful things to become permissible. The whole scenario will be considered. If an expert doctor was to state that there is no cure besides this unlawful substance, plus there is no other alternative and it is certain the life will be at risk, then only in such extreme circumstances consuming an unlawful substance for medical treatment would be permissible otherwise it will not be.

In short, there are three conditions for anyone to be permitted to intake or benefit from any unlawful substance;

1. To be in the state of Idhtirār whereby not using the unlawful substance, one's life is in danger.
2. It is for certain i.e. an expert doctor informs that this is undoubtedly the only cure for such illness.
3. No other alternative is available.

Contemporary Fiqh   Organ Transplantation

If anyone fulfils the above three conditions, then the jurists unanimously agree that it would be permissible to utilize an unlawful substance for medical treatment.

Is it permissible in the state of Hājat to utilise unlawful substances?

Having elaborated on the injunctions of Idhtirār in the terminology of Shari'ah, it is now apparent that only in extreme circumstances, where there is certainty of one being on the point of death and there is no other alternative, it would be permissible to utilize an unlawful substance. Almost all the jurists unanimously agree to this. Likewise, the whole scenario will be taken into consideration and merely having an apprehension of loss of life will be insufficient. This rule will be applied in all those cases where a person's life would be at risk, for instance, threatened, medical treatment etc.

A question now arises that in the case of Hājat, would it be permissible to use or benefit from unlawful substances?

As I have discussed earlier, Hājat is a state whereby a person's life is not at risk, as in the case of Idhtirār, but there is certainty that unless an unlawful substance is used, the health will extremely deteriorate. The state of Hājat makes one unable to carry out their daily work or duties properly due to their weakness of health.

In such circumstances, Islām has granted some concessions in wor-

Contemporary Fiqh   Organ Transplantation

ship. For example, if a person is unable to stand in Salāh, then he/ she may sit down and pray. Sitting will be a substitute for standing. If unable to sit, then one is granted the concession to lie down. Similarly, if one is not able to fast, then it would be permissible to break the fast and postpone it when a person recovers. This has been unanimously agreed by all of the jurists.

Nevertheless, there have been differences of opinion of whether a Hājat person is permitted to utilise or consume an unlawful substance to prevent his health from deteriorating. Many of the Jurists have adopted the view that it would be permissible to take benefit from unlawful substances in the case of Hājat when no other solution is available.

In support of this, the jurists have derived the ruling from a Hadīth which is related in Abū Dāwūd, Tirmizi and Nasai, that once Sayyidunā Urfah Ibn As'ad ﷺ participated in a battle and during the battle his nose was severed. The Sahābi ﷺ got an artificial nose made for himself out of silver but it used to cause him a lot of difficulty. He thus informed the Holy Prophet ﷺ about it. The Holy Prophet ﷺ instructed him to get an artificial nose made for himself out of gold and use it.

This Hadīth is authentic and many jurists have accepted its authenticity. In this Hadīth, the Sahābi ﷺ was instructed to wear an artificial nose made out of gold, whereas, gold is strictly prohibited for men. It is related in Nasai that once the Holy Prophet ﷺ emerged from his home where he had gold in one hand and silk

Contemporary Fiqh   Organ Transplantation

clothes in the other and stated, "These two items are prohibited for the men of my Ummah and permitted for the women of my Ummah." In spite of this, for medical treatment, the Holy Prophet ﷺ instructed the Sahābi ؓ to use a nose made out of gold. It is also apparent that this Sahābi ؓ was not on the point of death but was in extreme difficulty.

From this Hadīth, we come to know that in the state of Hājat it would be permissible to benefit from unlawful substances provided it is with the following conditions:

1. An expert doctor who is reliable, informs that in this unlawful substance there is cure and no other lawful substance can substitute it.
2. There is certainty and not apprehension.
3. There is no other alternative whatsoever.

If we were to analyze the Hadīth of Sayyidunā Urfah ؓ, we come to know that these conditions are deduced from this incident. The Holy Prophet ﷺ had ordered him to use a nose made out of gold and certainly the Holy Prophet ﷺ was an expert. The Holy Prophet ﷺ was also certain about it, otherwise, he would have not informed him. Lastly, the Sahābi ؓ resorted to other necessary means available at that time, which was why he primarily used an artificial nose made of silver but this did not solve the problem.

The jurists have stated the conditions as follows, "It is permitted to utilize it if one knows that there is cure in it and he knows no other cure for it." (Durrul Mukhtār)

Allāmah Shāmi ﷺ states in this regard, "It is permissible to take benefit (from such medicine) if one knows that there is cure in it and does not know of any other medicine." (Shāmi).

In summary, in the state of Hājat, it would also be permissible to use unlawful substances.

After understanding the abovementioned major points, we now come to the questions:

1. What is the Islamic ruling regarding blood transfusion?
Blood is vital for every human being and without it, a person cannot sustain life. At the same time, it is also impure and considered Najis. The issue of blood transfusion did not exist in the time of the Holy Prophet ﷺ, the time of the Sahābah ؓ or the generation after them. Therefore, the contemporary jurists have employed Ijtihād in this matter and used the analogical deduction with a woman's milk.

The milk of a woman is part of her body and it is imperative for her to feed her child when it requires it, within the period of two years. It is not required to cut up the limb to draw out milk but it is extracted by the child. It is not permissible for a man or a woman to drink the milk of a woman, unless it is for medical purposes. This is mentioned in Fatāwa Hindiyyah, "There is no harm for a man to drink the milk of a woman for medical treatment only."

Contemporary Fiqh   Organ Transplantation

Likewise, blood is also vital to sustain life. Blood can be drawn out by merely using a needle, without having to cut up any limb of the body. Unless it be for medical treatment, it would not be permissible to obtain blood from another person. The ruling of obtaining blood is somewhat similar to the ruling of obtaining a woman's milk for medical treatment. Therefore, blood transfusion for medical purpose would be permissible.

Nevertheless, the following conditions must be born in mind in order to obtain blood from someone:

a) Looking at the strict principles, it would not be permissible to utilize it or obtain it from anyone unless a person is in the state of Idhtirār (need). Furthermore, an expert Muslim doctor informs that this is the only solution to this problem.

b) Also with the exception of Hājat (there is no certainty of life in jeopardy but the health will extremely deteriorate) where an expert doctor informs that there is no other solution besides this, then it would be permissible to transfuse blood into someone else's body or obtain it from someone else.

2. Is organ transplant permissible?

In addition to blood, organs are also vital for every human being. The contemporary jurists unanimously agree that it is permissible to obtain an organ from an animal in the case of Idhtirār and Hājat. However, the jurists differ with regards to the permissibility of

Contemporary Fiqh   Organ Transplantation

surgically transferring an organ of a healthy person into an ill person.

The basis of the difference between the jurists is whether or not transplanting an organ into another person is a degradation of a human being's honour. This is because Allāh ﷻ has sanctified and honoured the status of a human being over many of his other creations. The jurists who prohibit organ transplants do so because it violates the honour of a human being and above all, every organ and limb belongs to Allāh ﷻ. Hence, they hold that no human being can employ it in any way he/she wishes.

On the other hand, some jurists, for instance Shaykh Khālid Saifullāh, agree to the permissibility of organ transplants, arguing that transferring an organ into another body in order to save a person's life is not an infringement of a human being's honour. In fact, to render an organ to save somebody's life is considered an act of honour and reverence as Allāh ﷻ states in the Holy Qur'ān, **"And whosoever saves a human being then it is as though he has saved the whole of humanity." (5:32)**

Shaykh Khālid Saifullāh further argues that although Allāh ﷻ has honoured and esteemed mankind, the Holy Qur'ān and the Ahādīth of the Holy Prophet ﷺ have not clearly set any boundaries of honour and neither have they explicitly mentioned them. In such cases, the jurists will refer to the custom affair, which in the terminology of Shari'ah is known as Urf or Ādat. This will be taken into consideration and some juristic issues can be deduced when it

Contemporary Fiqh   Organ Transplantation

is not categorically mentioned in the Holy Qur'ān or Hadīth .

Urf will be considered as long as it does not contradict the fundamental principles of Islām. The evidence of the reliability of Urf is mentioned in the Hadīth related in Musnad Ahmad that the Holy Prophet ﷺ said, "Whatever the Muslims consider to be good then that will be good in the eyes of Allāh ﷻ." Some jurists have mentioned that this Hadīth was not the words of the Holy Prophet ﷺ but stated by Sayyidunā Abdullāh Ibn Mas'ūd ﵁. Nevertheless, the jurists have accepted it.

In another Hadīth, it is related that the Holy Prophet ﷺ had prohibited all the bad and corrupt customs and instructed all the good customs (Hujjatullāhil Bālighah). However, if any custom contradicts the fundamental principles of Islām then all the jurists unanimously agree that such custom will not be accepted at any cost.

Customs and traditions vary from time to time by which different injunctions will be given to befit the time. The Shari'ah has not set any boundaries or limits on how and when a human being's esteem is violated. Hence, the time and the tradition will be taken into consideration.

Mufti Kifāyatullāh ﷫ states that at this present time, due to the progress of technology, new surgical methods of obtaining organs have emerged and in the society it is considered an honour to save someone's life. For this reason organ transplant should be permitted. (Kifāyatul Mufti)

Shaykh Khālid Saifullāh further argues that the jurists agree with the permissibility of blood transfusion in the state of Idhtirār and Hājat. The jurists do not regard it as an act of infringement of mankind's honour when blood in someone's body is being transferred into another person's, so how can organ transplants infringe the dignity of a person?

Another proof the jurists present for the permissibility of organ transplant is the principle:

$$ الضَّرُوْرَاتُ تُبِيْحُ الْمَحْظُوْرَاتِ $$

This means at the time of need (Idhtirār), prohibited things become permissible to use. This principle is deduced from the Holy Qur'ān where Allāh ﷻ states, **"But if anyone is forced by necessity without wilful disobedience or transgressing, then there is no sin." (2:173)**

In short, organ transplants are permitted in the case of Idhtirār and Hājat and in doing so, one will not be violating the honour and esteem of mankind. In fact, saving another human being's life is an honour itself. If in the state of Idhtirār and Hājat, blood transfusion is permitted, then organ transplant should also be permitted.

3. Is it permissible to use artificial limbs?
It would be permissible to use artificial limbs as it was in the case of Sayyidunā Urfah Ibn As'ad ؓ in the Hadīth mentioned where

he got an artificial nose for himself made of gold.

(Abū Dāwūd, Tirmizi and Nasai)

4. Is it permissible to donate an organ to someone who is in urgent need of it during his life or to make a will to donate an organ?

It would be permissible for a living person to donate an organ to someone who is in urgent need of it (i.e. in the state of Idhtirār and Hājat) provided that it is with the condition that the donor grants permission and by donating an organ, one will not suffer a major loss in life or health. For instance, one cannot donate a heart because a person cannot sustain life without a heart.

If the deceased made a will and granted permission during his/her life time to donate an organ and the deceased's legal inheritors also grant permission, then it would be permissible to obtain it from him/her. Furthermore, it is permissible for the deceased to make a will to donate an organ but only to a person who is in urgent need.

Allāh ﷻ Knows Best

The Islamic Perspective of Abortion
Dr Rafaqat Rashid

Q Abortion has now become an endemic problem amongst the Muslim community. Many Muslims are not aware of how serious this matter is nor are they aware of its Islamic guidelines. I would be very grateful if you could shed some light on this matter.

A Throughout history, all religions perceived abortion as an abhorrent evil. No moral distinction was made between an embryo, foetus or a baby. Hence, killing a foetus or embryo was considered no different from killing a newborn. Times have changed considerably. Individualism and self-interest have become a central driving factor in our life decisions. The interests of the parents override any interest in the moral status of an embryo or foetus. The liberal views of the modern world have had a great influence on Muslims, in terms of family planning issues related to contraception and even abortion.

The abortion laws in the UK have been relaxed gradually since their initiation. The strict laws against criminal abortion of 1861 were enforced until The Abortion Act of 1967, which laid a criteria for abortions based on risk of physical or mental injury to the pregnant women or substantial physical or mental abnormality to the foetus. The practice of abortion has gradually become such a common practice with the increasingly relaxed amendments that abortion on demand is now a reality. I have personally witnessed cases of married and unmarried Muslim women using abortion as a form of contraception. It is for this reason that I feel it necessary to educate the public on the ethical issues around abortion from the Islamic perspective.

The Moral Status of the Unborn
Islām holds the moral status of the unborn child very highly. Allāh ﷻ and His Messenger ﷺ have given such importance to the subject that a detailed account is given of the stages of the foetal growth, both in the Holy Qur'ān, in numerous places and the Ahādīth.

Sayyidunā Abdullāh Ibn Mas'ūd ؓ narrates that the Holy Prophet ﷺ stated, "Verily the creation of each one of you is brought together in his mother's womb for forty days in the form of Nutfa (drop of fluid), then he is an Alaqa (clot of blood) for a like period, then a Mudgha (lump of flesh) for a like period, then there is sent to him the angel who blows the breath of life into him." (Bukhāri, Muslim)

This Hadīth explains that the embryo-foetus goes through three stages of 40 days, each a total of 120 days, before the soul is breathed into it and it is then considered a person. Once the foetus has reached 120 days, it has a moral status similar to the newborn. These 120 days are to be counted from the time of fertilisation (conception) and therefore, are considered as approximately 19 weeks pregnancy according to antenatal recordings. According to medical science, by this stage, the bones of the child-to-be, are fully hardened, the final stages of preparation to survive outside the womb (i.e. strengthening of chest muscles) are in process and the foetus reacts and perceives stimulation inside and outside the womb. The child has hearing and visual perception and the heart responds to stimulation in rhythm.

Allāh ﷻ says, **"He then fashioned him in due proportion, and breathed into him something of His spirit (approximately 120 days). And He gave you (the faculties of) hearing and sight and feeling (and understanding), little thanks do you give"** [32:9]

When Does Islām Permit Abortion in Serious Cases?

Abortion, at all times is generally not permissible and would be considered killing a potential human species, yet, different schools of thought vary in their opinion as to when it would be excused in serious cases. Out of the four Sunni Schools, the Hanafi School is the most liberal in terms of the window of opportunity given to abort. According to the Hanafi School, abortion beyond 120 days would be impermissible as this is after ensoulment and the moral status of the foetus is now that of a person. Some of the jurists of the Shāfi'ī School also agree with 120 days and others have the more conservative view of 40 days only. The Hanbali School also considers 40 days as the maximum days before which one can legitimately abort if there is a qualified need. Finally, the Māliki School do not allow qualified abortion in either periods.

What Qualifies for Legitimate Abortion in Islām?

I shall only deal with the Hanafi School as space does not permit me to go into further detail. Qualified cases for justified abortions are at three levels. Those that relate to the foetus, those that relate to the mother and those that relate to society at large. (Note that according to the Hanafi School, abortion beyond 120 days would not be permissible).

Foetal Reasons: Severe disabilities or disease conditions that significantly reduce quality of life because of functional demand, pain and suffering. For example, serious suffering (i.e. full blown thalasaemia) or serious functional deformity (i.e. anencephaly).

Maternal Reasons: Significant danger to mother's physical or mental health or hard cases of incest or rape. Illegitimate intercourse (Zinā) will not qualify for abortion as the cause of such a pregnancy is blameworthy.

Societal Reasons: Reproductive technologies (i.e. IVF) as treatment for infertility only, where remaining embryos can be discarded after finding a suitable one.

Note: Above 120 days, abortion is only permissible in cases of necessity, which are emergency cases of real/certain and immediate need, such as, when one must choose between the life of the mother or the foetus.

Penalty for Illegal Abortion
If abortion is performed illegitimately for whatever reason, then according to the Hanafi School, a Diya (blood money for taking a human life) is given if abortion is performed after 120 days. A Ghurra (1/20th of Diya) is to be given if the abortion is performed prior to 120 days and human characteristics are visible.

Death Rites of the Aborted

If the foetus is less than 120 days, it is not considered a human and is therefore, not given a name, no Ghusl or Kafan is given and it is buried without Janāzah. However, if there are signs of limb formation and one can see formed fingers, nails, hairs etc, then Ghusl is performed, a name is given, the foetus is wrapped in a cloth without Kafan and Janāzah is not performed. It is important that the foetus is buried. It is important that you do this promptly, especially for "non-viable foetuses", because if you do not, then the hospital will make arrangements for disposal/burial. If the child is over 120 days and is stillborn and it is difficult to determine the sex of the child, then a neutral name suitable for both boys and girls should be given.

Conclusion

Abortion is no simple matter in Islām at any time of pregnancy and is forbidden without a legitimate Shar'ī reason. Those who perform abortion for illegitimate reasons such as, discovering that the foetus is a female, or any other unqualified reason, will be accountable before Allāh ﷻ and before the potential person they denied a life to.

"Kill not your children for fear of want, We provide sustenance for them and for you, the killing of them is a great sin." [17:31]

"And when the girl-child who was buried alive is asked, 'For what sin she was slain?'" [81:8-9]

Finally, it is important to note that this article is brief and does not present answers to individual cases as each case is different and has its own complexities. Therefore, one must discuss such an important issue with a Mufti who has knowledge in this area.

Allāh ﷻ Knows Best

Medicine and Food Containing Harām Ingredients
Dr Rafaqat Rashid

Q I was told that a lot of the medication that is prescribed by doctors is Harām. This is really concerning. Can you explain how true this is and discuss how Muslims should deal with this issue?

A I am a real believer of facts and research. To answer your question, I will outline a research that was carried out on 50 Muslim patients who used a community pharmacy in a West Midlands inner-city location in 2001. A self completion questionnaire was presented; all 50 patients completed the questionnaire as well as 18 Muslim GPs (53% of total Muslim GPs who were asked to complete the questionnaire). The results were as follows:

100% of Muslim patients and Muslim GPs stated that they tried to eat and drink Halāl items only.

13% of Muslim patients indicated that they would take a medication if they were unsure of whether it was Halāl or not.

42% of Muslim patients indicated that they would not take any medication that they were not sure was Halāl.

58% of Muslim patients indicated that they would stop taking a medication if they found out that it was Harām.

8% of Muslim patients and **22%** of Muslim GPs felt that it was acceptable for Muslim patients to take Harām medication for a minor illness or disease.

36% of Muslim patients and **44%** of Muslim GPs felt that it was acceptable for Muslim patients to take Harām medication for a major illness or disease.

50% of Muslim patients believed that their doctor was aware of the needs of Harām and Halāl medication.

64% of Muslim patients and **56%** of Muslim GPs indicated that Muslims could not, or that they were unsure, as to whether they could take Harām medication for treating major illnesses.

[A. Bashir, M. Asif; Pharmacy Practice Research Group, Aston University, Aston Triangle. Int J Pharm Pract 2001:9suppl:(R78)]

The conclusions I would draw from this questionnaire are that most Muslim GPs are quite unaware about the rulings related to Harām medication. Secondly, that the majority of Muslim patients do not challenge their GPs on these issues or make enquiries. As a result, there is a lot of ignorance regarding Harām/Halāl medication and the indications for their use. Finally, we have to be honest and accept that there are not that many practicing Muslim GPs in the medical profession (though this is increasing) and that some patients just simply do not care, or are too embarrassed to make enquiries. The solution is that greater awareness, research and education are needed for all parties, doctors, patients and Imāms.

Giving verdicts on whether a certain medication is permissible or not depends on each circumstance and individual, in some cases. To take a general Fatwa and expect all to act on that Fatwa could be potentially dangerous, especially in serious circumstances where a particular medication is important but not understood to be by the patient. My suggestion is that patients should seek help from qualified scholars who have an understanding of the issues related to that circumstance.

To demonstrate the complexity of the knowledge required and the different circumstances that the scholars have to deal with to pass a Fatwa, I will list some of the common juristic principles that are used, based upon the purposes of Shari'ah (Maqāsid As-Shari'ah), in identifying whether certain Harām medications can be used. Two principles (Maqāsid adh-Dharūriyya) would include:

1) Preservation of life (Hifz an-Nafs).
2) Preservation of intellect (Hifz al-Aql).

In order to preserve both these principles the rule of necessity applies, i.e. necessities make prohibition lawful.

Other important principles are:

- Cases of need are restricted to the actual need.

- That which becomes permissible due to a justifying circumstance, will become impermissible again with the disappearance of the justifying circumstance.

- Total transformation or essential transformation of the Harām ingredient.

- Common affliction/ordeal.

I will begin by listing and briefly explaining the more common Harām ingredients that are used in everyday medication. The main group of drugs/medication of public interest are categorised as:

- Gelatine-based.
- Alcohol containing products.
- Inactive ingredients derived from possible animal sources.

Gelatine

A protein produced by partial hydrolysis of collagen (skins, tendons, ligaments, bones, cartilages and hooves) extracted from connective tissues of animals such as the domesticated bovines (cattle), porcines (pig, swine) and equines (horse). The worldwide production amount of gelatine is about 300,000 tons per year (roughly 600 million lbs). On a commercial scale, gelatine is made from byproducts of the meat and leather industry which is mainly pork skins, pork and cattle bones, or split cattle hides. The name "gelatine" is colloquially applied to all types of gels and jellies but properly used, it currently refers solely to the animal protein product. Gelatine typically constitutes the shells of medicine capsules in order to make them easier to swallow. Hypromellose is the vegetarian counterpart to gelatine, but is more expensive to produce. A very important note to make is that some tablets also contain gelatine not just capsules (even certain paracetamol tablets).

Contemporary Fiqh — Harām in Food and Medicine

The scholars explain that because it is commonly derived from pork, unlawful animals or animals not Islamically slaughtered, it is impure and Harām. If there is no doubt that it is derived from a Halāl source, then it is Halāl. If there is doubt, then it will still be considered Harām and should be avoided.

As in any ingredient, if it is derived from an unlawful animal (source) i.e. pork or an animal not Islamically slaughtered and it is known through extensive research, without a doubt, that the ingredient undergoes such a change that it retains no properties of its former state, then it will become pure, thus, permissible to use. Most Hanafi jurists therefore, consider gelatine as Harām because there is doubt, or it is difficult to establish where it is derived from. Secondly, the change it undergoes from its original state is not sufficient to be considered essential transformation and therefore, it is considered Harām. However, the Hanafi jurists allow the use of impure and unlawful substances for medical purposes, provided certain conditions are met.

The Hanafi jurist, Imām al-Haskafi ﷺ says, "The scholars differed regarding the usage of Harām medication. The apparent opinion in the (Hanafi) school is that it is Harām. However, it is said that it will be permissible when the medicine is known to be effective and there is no other alternative, just as there is a dispensation in drinking alcohol for a person dying of thirst and the Fatwa is given on this opinion." (Durrul-Mukhtār)

In view of the above text from one of the fundamental Hanafi ref-

Contemporary Fiqh   Harām in Food and Medicine

erence books, it will be permissible to use medicines that have impure and unlawful substances in them, provided the following conditions are met:

1) It is reasonably known that the medicine will be effective and is needed.

2) There is no permissible reasonably available alternative (taking into consideration availability, significant cost implications or other genuine issues such as what is tolerated by the patient).

3) These two factors have been established by a qualified Muslim doctor who is at least outwardly upright and God-fearing (or inquiring with an experienced specialist, who genuinely sympathises with these values, if the Muslim doctor is not available).

So, as one can gather from the above Fatwas, although the substance being used is classified by the Shari'ah ruling as Harām, it can be used for medicinal purposes with the conditions mentioned and can differ for different patients and circumstances.

Gelatine Capsules

Production of medicine is determined by factors such as form, cost, stability, particle size, taste, slow release, etc. If a product is very bitter or can cause irritation or damage to the lining of the mouth, it may be concealed in a capsule form which when swallowed will release its contents either in the stomach or the gut depending on the capsule type. There are currently 3 types of material used to formulate capsules for the purpose of delivery of the medication:

1) Hard gelatine
2) Soft gelatine
3) A cellulose derivative derived from plant extracts

In the majority of cases, the gelatine used is derived from animal sources for both hard and soft capsules as this is the cheapest and the most readily available form. The gelatine derived from vegetable sources is less commonly used in the pharmaceutical field due to cost implications. Such capsules are labelled "suitable for vegetarians". In general all capsules that are hard or soft gelatine are not labelled as "suitable for vegetarians" and should be assumed to be of animal origin.

Pharmaceutically, when there is an equivalent product available (i.e. in liquid form), it becomes the responsibility of the Muslim doctor, pharmacist, dispenser and the patient to ensure that this is made aware so that the appropriate action can be taken depending on the circumstance. The reality is that the patient has greater influence on making the change as he is the one who has the greater influence on the prescriber. The patient should ideally discuss this with his doctor so that the right alternative medication can be prescribed.

Pharmacists cannot substitute the medication to a Halāl alternative without the consent of the prescriber (i.e. doctor). It is a fact that not many Muslim doctors are aware of the minor ingredients which are used in the production of most medications and sometimes, it can be difficult and expensive for the prescriber to find an alternative. Therefore, the pharmacist can be used to determine this. A practical solution to this is if a doctor prescribes amoxicillin capsules (antibiotic), the patient can ask the doctor to write a prescription for amoxicillin suspension instead. It is also worthwhile informing the doctor to put this on the patient's medical records so as to save future misunderstandings.

Patients have tried to open up the capsule and swallow the contents. Most of the time this is not problematic, especially for most short term medication but it can cause issues such as:

1) It may not be easy to break open the capsule without losing some of its contents.

2) The contents may taste bitter and trying to consume the dry powder may prove difficult. Some patients drink it in a glass of water or sprinkle it in a sandwich.

3) The contents of the capsule may irritate the lining of the tongue and mouth or cause slight damage.

4) Some of these capsules are manufactured with a coating for pharmacological reasons not just for preservation etc. A medication may be encapsulated for the purpose of modified release or control release suited for that patients needs (it can be released slowly and absorbed at a later stage in the gut). Therefore, the

effectiveness of the medication may be reduced. I would advise seeking medical advice regarding this from the pharmacist.

Alcohol and Medicine

From my experience, understanding the Islamic rulings about alcohol containing products has always confused the masses. It is true that there are differences of opinion on the conditions of use of alcohol containing products. Unfortunately, it is without doubt that there are a lot of common medical suspensions (liquid medication) containing alcohol of some type. This has always caused confusion about which alcohol is permissible and which is Harām? Another point to note is that the majority of topical medications (creams, ointments, sprays) also contain alcohol. This may also include antiseptic wipes or even common household detergents/ antiseptics. The reality is that we are surrounded by alcohol containing products in the form of either food, medication, cleansing liquids, body applications and virtually any other liquid that is useful!

So what do the Islamic jurists say regarding these products? I shall first briefly outline the differences of opinion between the different Islamic scholars and then, what the contemporary Islamic scholars conclude from this, explaining a little detail of what type of alcohol is actually not considered 'Khamr' or is not Harām. Then I will present some easy practical points on how we should deal with alcohol containing medication/products.

Contemporary Fiqh   Harām in Food and Medicine

Differences of Opinion of the Classical Jurists

Firstly, there is a difference of opinion between the scholars of the Hanafi Fiqh. Imām Abū Hanīfah 🕮, Imām Abū Yusūf 🕮 (Shaykhain) were of the opinion that it will not be permissible to consume alcohol of the 'Ashribah Arba' (i.e. grape juice, processed grape juice, dried grape (raisins) juice and date juice), but those alcohols derived from other than this, can be consumed for genuine purposes or for medicinal reasons, as long as it is not used for recreational purposes. This is with the condition that it does not intoxicate the person consuming this alcohol. This would be permissible, even in cases without the rule of necessity.

The other main jurist of the Hanafi Fiqh, Imām Muhammad 🕮, along with Imām Shāfi'ī 🕮, Imām Mālik 🕮 and Imām Ahmad 🕮 differ and state that all alcohol (including that which is not of the 'Ashribah Arba') is Harām and considered impure, no matter what the quantity, small or big.

In one of the most relied upon sources for Hanafi Fiqh, 'Shāmi,' Imām Ibn Ābidīn al-Haskafi states that the Hanafi Fatwa is on the position of Imām Muhammad 🕮 that all alcohol is Harām and impure, no matter how small a quantity because of widespread Fitna (tribulation). This is also the position held by the other three Imāms (i.e. Imām Shāfi'ī 🕮, Imām Mālik 🕮 and Imām Ahmad 🕮) due to the Hadīth , "Every intoxicant is Khamr and every intoxicant is unlawful (Harām)," (Muslim) and also the Hadīth , "Whatever intoxicates in large quantities, then a small quantity of it is also forbidden," (Ahmad, Ibn Mājah and Dār-Qutni). The (Hanafi) scholars

Contemporary Fiqh

Harām in Food and Medicine

have stated that the Fatwa of prohibition given in our times is due to widespread Fitna, meaning that due to the fact that most people now consume these beverages for the purpose of pleasure and not to gain strength for worship, they have been forbidden altogether. (Raddul Muhtār alā-Durrul Mukhtār)

What Do Contemporary Islamic Jurists Say?

Due to the difference of opinion of Imām Abū Hanīfah ﷺ and Imām Abū Yūsuf ﷺ, contemporary scholars have ruled that the consumption of alcohol-containing products/food is permissible for medical purposes/energy and the prevalent perfumes, deodorants and creams may be used, as long as the alcohol used in them is from other than grapes, dates or Ethyl alcohol (ethanol).

The contemporary Hanafi jurist, Mufti Muhammad Taqi Uthmāni states:

"The explanation given for the ruling of alcohol, the usage of which has become so widespread that it is used in many medicines, perfumes and other products, is that if the alcohol is taken from grapes or dates, then this is not permissible or pure. If the alcohol is derived from other than grapes or dates, then there is no problem in taking the view of Imām Abū Hanīfah ﷺ, in that it will not be considered unlawful to use such alcohol for medicinal reasons or for other legitimate purposes, as long as the alcohol does not reach the level of intoxication since it is not regarded impure according to Imām Abū Hanīfah ﷺ. The alcohol used today in medicines, perfumes and other than that is not taken from grapes and dates, rather it is derived from grains, peels and petroleum etc." (Takmila Fathul-Mulhim Sharh Sahīh Muslim)

To make sense of these rulings we need to understand what 'Khamr' actually is. According to the Hanafi jurists, the Arabic word 'Khamr', as mentioned in the Holy Qur'ān, means specifically, that intoxicant made from grapes because it was the common practice in those days to make alcohol from grapes. This is not to say that alcohol derived from other sources is not Harām. The Jurists agree that intoxicants made from dates, wheat and barley would also come into this category of Harām.

Due to Umūmul Balwa (the widespread use of alcohol in virtually all liquid products), it has been proven to be quite difficult to avoid alcohol containing products. It is for this reason that our contemporary Hanafi scholars have stated that alcohol containing products, other than those derived from grapes and dates are **permissible for external use** and are not Harām. Synthetic alcohols (other than ethyl alcohol/ethanol) are considered pure and are permitted to use and consume under the following conditions (supported by verdicts in Fatāwa Alamghīri):

1. They are not used as intoxicants (i.e. for recreational purposes, even a little).

2. They are not used in amounts that intoxicate.

3. They are not used in Lahw (vain) without real need.

So Which Alcohol is Halāl?

Just to clarify an important point which is sometimes confused and can be misunderstood, is the nature of synthetic alcohol. As the name suggests it has **not** been extracted from the fruits such as grapes, dates etc. but it is synthesised chemically.

Cetyl alcohol is a long chain synthesised alcohol which is solid. Hence, obviously it is not drinkable nor does it cause intoxication if at all ingested. Therefore, it is Halāl to use in cosmetic products. It is also not absorbed through the skin when applied as a cream.

Fruits such as dates and grapes when they ferment, produce **Ethyl alcohol,** the intoxicating agent which is a short chain alcohol (C2 H5 OH) (a liquid which is also produced industrially by ethylene (gas) dehydration and by petroleum sources). Therefore, even if it is synthesised chemically, it will be considered intoxicating because it has the same chemical formula and the same quality of intoxication. Therefore, it is not different scientifically, in its structure, property and quality, from alcohol obtained from the fermentation method of grapes and dates.

It is commonly used as a solvent in natural and artificial flavours and in the production of cosmetics and intermediates in the manufacture of other chemicals. It is also used as an extracting solvent in vanilla products such as vanilla extract (about 35%) in many cosmetic agents both for men (aftershave lotion) and for female perfumes. Ethyl alcohol is absorbed through the skin. It then passes through the flesh into the blood vessels and finally mixes with the blood and circulates throughout the body. Therefore all liquid cosmetic products containing Ethyl alcohol are not permissible. Other names given to synthetic Ethyl alcohol are, Ethanol and Methylated Spirits (contains 5 percent Methyl alcohol and 95 percent Ethyl alcohol). Products containing these ingredients therefore, will also be prohibited.

They are Not the Same Thing!

Another important fact is the difference between Synthetic Ethyl alcohol and Denatured Ethyl alcohol. Denatured Ethyl alcohol can be made from Synthetic alcohol and also from Ethyl alcohol produced through fermentation method. But what we must understand is that the denaturation of ethanol is the act of rendering Ethyl alcohol unfit for beverage use by addition of substances known as denaturants (i.e. methanol). An example is the process of introducing Benzene during the distillation process. This leads to a chemical process where water is separated from the ethanol (Ethyl alcohol) producing denatured alcohol. Sometimes the ethanol is intensively denatured and that it becomes unfit for consumption. It is also important to note that the denaturant is not easily separable from the ethanol. Denatured alcohols lose their intoxicant qualities because of the addition of the denaturant to the ethanol. For this reason, the use of this in products would be permissible (i.e. cosmetics and domestic products).

Therefore it would be permitted to use the various types of perfumes, deodorants and creams that contain alcohol due to the fact that the alcohol contained in them is from other than grapes and dates, or it is a Synthetic alcohol (formulated from chemical substances other than Ethyl alcohol/ethanol) and not the Khamr that is absolutely impermissible.

However, it is more Taqwa (religiously precautionary) to avoid using such perfumes and deodorants, whenever reasonably possible because of the differences of opinion regarding it, though there will be no sin on that person.

I will finish by summarising some important facts relating to this article:

Summary and Practical Points:

1. Alcoholic beverages in all varieties and forms are unlawful for Muslims. This includes all types of wines, liquors, fermented beverages, pure alcohol and the like.

2. If it is known that a particular food contains alcohol derived from one of the four sources ('Ashribah Arba') (raw grape juice, processed grape juice, dried grape (raisins) juice and date juice) or it contains ethanol (Ethyl alcohol), then this food will not be permissible. Alcohol can be found in some Halāl foods, such as bread and soy sauce and this is usually not labelled. These sometimes contain minute amounts of alcohol as a result of a natural reaction between certain chemicals during the manufacturing process (without the intention of deliberately adding to add flavour), and

Contemporary Fiqh   Harām in Food and Medicine

so could not be classed as Harām. It should be noted that only Ethyl alcohol (such as methylated spirits and ethanol-the alcohol found in alcoholic drinks) are intoxicating and are therefore, Harām.

3. If it is known with certainty that a medicine contains alcohol derived from one of the four sources or ethanol, then such medicine is not permissible, except in times of necessity which are decided upon by a competent Muslim doctor, when there are no other alternatives.

4. Regarding medicine, the usage of such medicine in limitation will be allowed, if it is known with certainty that alcohol derived from other than the four sources and ethanol have been used as ingredients in that medication. (i.e. certain cough linctuses, certain mouth washes/sprays/gels etc.). According to Imām Abū Hanīfah ☙ and Imām Abū Yūsuf ☙, it will be permissible to use such medication providing it does not intoxicate.

5. If the Harām alcohol undergoes significant chemical changes (Tabdīlul Māhiyah), causing it to lose its original properties and is transformed after the process until it no longer remains alcohol, then all the Imāms agree to its usage and consumption, citing the case where wine turns into vinegar, losing all its former properties thus, making it permissible for Muslims because of the change of the original properties of wine.

6. It is permissible to use alcohol containing products such as after-shaves, deodorants, perfumes, creams etc., as long as these products are not derived from grapes, dates or ethanol. Products containing this will be considered impure, making both body and clothes impure.

Allāh ﷻ Knows Best

Sterilisation

Dr Rafaqat Rashid

Q **Dear Dr. Sāhib, Alhamdulillāh, I have just had my 7th child and my GP has advised me to have my 'tubes tied' (sterilised). I am finding it very difficult to cope with the kids and my health is not what it used to be. I do not think I will be able to manage if I have any more kids. What should I do?**

A There are a couple of things that need to be addressed regarding your situation. Primarily, what are your husband's thoughts regarding this? It is important that this is discussed with your husband as he has a right to decide, with mutual agreement, what would be the best option.

Raising seven children is not an easy affair and is physically, mentally and psychologically demanding. The Ulamā are agreed upon the view that the Islamic upbringing of children is an Islamic obligation and taking out time to nurture them is essential. For this reason, using contraception is permissible with the intention that one wishes to focus on the children's upbringing.

Sterilisation is an irreversible form of contraception through which one is unlikely ever to be fertile again. Therefore, sterilisation is unanimously agreed to be Harām (impermissible). Reversible contraception is permissible in such a situation. My advice to you would be to opt for either the contraceptive injection or the implant. The reasons for this is that they are both longer acting and do not require you to take daily tablets, which can be difficult for a

| Contemporary Fiqh | Sterilisation |

busy mother who has a lot on her mind. The usual contraceptive pill, the combined pill, contains two hormones, oestrogen and progestogen. Taken together in the pill, they prevent egg production in the women's ovaries. The implants and injections that are available in the UK contain only one hormone, progestogen. This makes them safer for some women who cannot take oestrogen. Like the pill they prevent egg production and so are very effective as contraceptives.

If you opt for the contraceptive injection, the doctor or a nurse will administer the injection in the muscle of your upper arm, buttocks or thigh. The injection lasts for 10 to 13 weeks (approximately 3 months), after which time, you must have another injection to maintain the contraceptive benefits. Some of the possible side effects of this form of contraception are slight weight gain and irregular vaginal bleeding in a few women. This has the potential of interfering with ones Salāh. One will also need to make regular 3 monthly scheduled appointments for repeated injections. It will also take several months before you have a normal menstrual cycle (periods) and become fertile again if stopped.

The other option is the implant. This works in the same manner as the injection and is the same hormone. It is a very small flexible rod that is placed just under your skin in your upper arm. It is a very effective, long-term hormonal method of contraception which protects you from pregnancy for up to 3-5 years. Like the injection, it can cause irregular menstruation in some women and slight changes in the weight which varies with individuals. If the implant is taken out, it is likely that the person will resume normal periods within a few months.

Another option, which may be mentioned is the Intrauterine Device (IUD) or the coil. The Islamic perspective is that this should ideally be avoided, as its permissibility is doubtful, because it can stop a fertilised egg from implanting in the womb, which is considered an early abortion and is therefore Harām.

Allāh ﷻ Knows Best

Caesarean

Dr Rafaqat Rashid

Q **I have had three Caesarean Sections. I have heard it is dangerous for me to have any more children. Is this true?**

A Some of the more common questions I am asked regarding Caesarean Sections (CS) are usually the one you have asked and whether it is safe to have a normal vaginal birth if one has had a previous CS.

To answer your question, there is concern that multiple caesareans lead to a weaker womb scar and that risk of this scar rupturing is therefore increased. Fortunately, there is very little research evidence to support this theory and an article appearing in the British Medical Journal in 1991 concluded this fact. (Roberts, Lawrence W; British Journal of Obstetrics and Gynaecology, December 1991, vol. 98, pg. 1199-1202)

The truth is, there is no set limit on the number of caesareans that can be carried out on an individual woman. The first caesarean is generally quite straightforward but as the number of caesareans increase, the more complicated the operation can become because of adhesions (scar tissue) from previous procedures. The issue here is not the womb rupturing during pregnancy or whilst giving birth, rather, it is how complicated the caesarean procedure may become with multiple operations. Many women have found themselves put under pressure to be sterilised because they have had several cae-

Contemporary Fiqh — Sterilisation

sareans. This is not permissible from an Islamic perspective and unethical from the western ethical viewpoint.

Many women are told that if they have already had two or more caesareans, that any future babies will need to be delivered by repeat caesarean. Evidence suggests that after one caesarean section, normal vaginal birth is widely accepted as safe. However, after two or more caesareans, it is normal protocol for a mother to be listed for an elective (planned) caesarean, since it is believed that the risks of caesarean scar rupture increase with the number of caesarean operations. Again, there is lack of evidence to support this view and for this reason, more researchers and obstetricians are questioning the basis for this protocol. (Enkin, M, Keirse, MJ NC, Renfrew, M and Neilson, 1995: "The Guide to Effective Care in Pregnancy and Childbirth" 2nd Edition. Oxford University Press, pg. 4l, 288)

In summary, if you have had 3 caesareans already and wish to have more children, there is no significant danger in you having more children. If you wish to have a normal vaginal birth after 3 caesareans, then there is no significant evidence to suggest that this could be dangerous. However, unfortunately, this is not the commonly accepted protocol by most obstetricians and therefore, chances are, you will be discouraged from this.

Allāh ﷻ Knows Best

Swine Flu Vaccine

Dr Rafaqat Rashid

Q Should Muslims take the Swine Flu vaccine as I have heard that it contains Harām ingredients?

A There are many opinions related to this subject but unfortunately, very few have actually spent time researching the subject. For Muslims the question arises whether Islamic considerations permit the use of the Swine Flu vaccines.

The following considerations have been given attention by Muslims:

1. Can we use preventative (prophylactic) therapy?
2. Can we use the source of the illness as a form of therapy?
3. Do Swine Flu vaccines contain Harām ingredients?
4. What are the conditions and limits of the use of Swine Flu vaccines?

1. Can we use preventative (prophylactic) therapy?

The answer to this question is evident in the following three Ahādīth:

1. Seeking that which benefits and that which reduces or ceases harm is encouraged. "The strong believer is better and more beloved to Allāh ﷻ than the weak Muslim and in everyone there is goodness, so seek that which will benefit you." (Muslim)

2. Using active therapy for preventative means is encouraged. "Whoever eats seven dates of Madīnah in the morning will not be harmed by witchcraft or poison." (Bukhāri)

3. Prevention of disease is not a negation of trust in Allāh ﷻ. "If you hear of a plague in a place, do not go there; and if it occurs where you are, do not leave such a place." (Bukhāri)

2. Can we use the source of the illness as a form of therapy?
Sayyidunā Abū Hurairah ؓ narrates from the Holy Prophet ﷺ, "If a house fly falls in the drink of anyone of you, he should dip it (in the drink), for one of its wings has a disease and the other has the cure for the disease." (Bukhāri)

Shāh Waliullāh Ad-Dihlawi ؓ mentioned in his book, Hujjatullāhil -Bālighah that, this Hadīth shows God-given knowledge of the many diseases a fly potentially carries as well as illustrates the Creator's wisdom in giving every venomous species some immunity or antidotal protection to its own poison, insuring its survival.

This suggests that Muslims can use the source of the illness (i.e. a viral strain of the Swine Flu virus) as a form of therapy (i.e. vaccines). As a matter of fact, variolation, the early technique of vaccination was introduced into England by Lady Mary Wortley Montagu after she had seen this being a regular practice in Ottoman Turkey in 1721.

3. Do Swine Flu vaccines contain Harām ingredients? This is the big question!

The following is a list of Swine Flu vaccines manufactured for Europe mentioning whether Harām constituents have been used in the process of production.

1. Pandermix (GSK vaccine) - grown in egg protein and splitting of the monovalent is done with sodium deoxycholate, which is derived from bovine bile. This is used in its production but is not in the final product. There are no porcine ingredients. Therefore, the final vaccine is Halāl.

2. Celvapen (Baxter vaccine) - grown in vero-cells - extracted from monkey kidney. Some porcine products are used in the manufacturing process of the Baxter vaccine (trypsin). However, there are no detectable traces of these products in the vaccine itself. Therefore, the final vaccine is Halāl.

3. Medimmune (nasal spray) - this contains 2mg/dose pork gelatine and is therefore, not permissible and is Harām.

Just to clarify the permissibility of the top two vaccines Pandermix and Celvapen, I refer to a valuable statement: "Claims have been made that various substances used to support the growth of viruses used in vaccines are present in the final vaccine product. This is untrue and is akin to saying there are trees in apple juice, just because the apples originated on trees. In the case of vaccines, viruses are grown initially in cell lines of various types. Then the

| Contemporary Fiqh | Swine Flu Vaccine |

viruses are harvested and go through multiple processing and purification steps over months of time before the final product is ready for use." (Pharmaceutical Research and Manufacturers of America).

4. What are the conditions & limits of the use of Swine Flu vaccines?

An essential rule in Islām is that any effort in preventing the harm of a source (i.e. Swine Flu) must be made, so as not to cause a greater or significant harm by neglecting that which is used to reduce this harm (i.e. Swine Flu vaccine). Islām makes clear that **harm must be eliminated** and **there must be no harm or reciprocating harm.** The parameters are whether we do nothing and use practical preventative measures (i.e. better sanitation and risk reducing behaviour) to reduce the seriousness of Swine Flu, or that we use vaccinations, or both. If the vaccinations are quite safe and have no significant dangerous adverse effects, then there is no issue regarding their permissibility. However, if the vaccination is of significant harm, then in Islām it will be justified on the premise that **a greater harm (i.e. Swine Flu) is eliminated by (tolerating) a lesser harm (i.e. the Swine Flu vaccine).**

Swine Flu Vaccines are Safe

The most common Swine Flu vaccine used in the UK is Pandemrix. Its minor adverse effects such as headache, tiredness, pain, redness, swelling or a hard lump at the injection site, fever, aching muscles joint pain and flu-like symptoms are quite common. Its serious effects such as allergic reactions of anaphylaxis, fits, severe arm pain are rare, with vasculitis and Guillain–Barré syndrome being extremely rare. The vaccine is in current use and several thousands of people have been vaccinated by it with no serious effects or deaths having being recorded.

There are Safety Measures in Place to Prevent Harm Which are Transparent for All to See!

Pandemrix (GSK) and Focetria (Novartis) were approved by The Committee for Medicinal Products for Human Use (CHMP) of the **European Medicines Agency** on 25 September 2009 and Celvapen (Baxter) was approved the following week.

"Assessments conducted by CHMP are based on purely scientific criteria and determine whether or not the products concerned meet the necessary quality, safety and efficacy requirements (in accordance with EU legislation, particularly Directive 2001/83/EC). These processes ensure that medicinal products have a positive risk-benefit balance in favour of patients/users of these products, once they reach the marketplace...The CHMP publishes a European Public Assessment Report (EPAR) for every centrally authorised product that is granted a marketing authorisation, setting out the scientific grounds for the Committee's opinion in favour of granting the authorization."

(EMEA website) This, as well as a regular update for anyone to scrutinize, is accessible to all i.e. for pandermix at:

http://www.emea.europa.eu/influenza/vaccines/pandemrix/ pandemrix_pi.html

Have the Vaccines Been Properly Tested?

The vaccines are new but are very similar to existing H5N1 flu vaccines that GSK and Baxter have already developed. They have been used on millions of people over the past years. The only difference is the different strain of virus, which does not substantially affect the safety profile of the vaccines. Two thousand people received GSK's H1N1 swine flu vaccine in clinical trials before its authorisation. This demonstrated that the H1N1 adjuvant vaccine is similar in its tolerability profile to the previously EMEA approved H5N1 adjuvant flu vaccines. Extensive trials give confidence that the new Swine Flu vaccines carry a very low risk and high protection rate (70-80%) and as such, they have now been licensed for use in 27 European countries.

Conclusion

It has been shown that Islām encourages preventative strategies to overcome harm by using preventative (prophylactic) therapy. Prevention at the source of the illness, as a form of therapy, is also permitted. The Swine Flu vaccines currently used in the UK contain no Harām ingredients in the final product and are therefore, permissible.

Clear evidence shows that they are the most effective means of reducing harm from Swine Flu and cause no substantial harm. This is supported by the fact that thousands are currently vaccinated and no substantial harm has been evident. There are many websites and much literature present that have an anti-vaccination agenda. They scaremonger the general public by trying to show that vaccines do not work, they weaken or overload the immune system, they cause autism, autoimmune diseases like diabetes, asthma, arthritis, crohns disease, MS, long term chronic neurological disorders, AIDS, cancer and sudden infant death syndrome or that they contain toxic ingredients. All these statements are false, manipulative and dishonest. For those who are not convinced, I would recommend the following articles: (reference 3). The Final conclusion is that Swine Flu vaccinations are permissible and should be encouraged at this stage for all "at risk" groups.

Allāh ﷻ Knows Best

Smoking Shīsha (Water-Pipe Tobacco Smoking)
By Mufti Abdul Waheed

Q Smoking Shīsha has become a common trend among many Muslims of today, just as smoking cigarettes. According to latest research, smoking Shīsha is associated to severe health issues. I would like to know the Islamic viewpoint regarding smoking Shīsha .

A Smoking Shīsha or opening Shīsha bars has become a widespread problem within the Muslim community. Smoking Shīsha is not only detrimental to oneself but also to the society. Therefore, it is necessary to address this issue in order to raise awareness for the general public of its harmful effects, physically and socially and its true Islamic position. After a careful scrutiny of this issue in terms of its harmful effects and evil social impact and the evidences in light of the Holy Qur'ān and Hadīth, the Fatwa in our times should be ruled as Harām or at least Makrūh-e-Tahrīmi. Both of these terms denote prohibition and unlawfulness and the one who smokes Shīsha or provides Shīsha, will become sinful in the eyes of Allāh ﷻ.

It is the norm of every man and woman that whenever he/she perceives a thing as pleasurable, he/she tends to ignore its harmful effects as the Holy Prophet ﷺ rightfully said, "Your love for (pleasurable) things blinds you and deafens you." (Abū Dāwūd, Ahmad) Mulla Ali Qāri ﷺ states regarding this Hadīth, that 'blinds you' refers to not being able to see its harmful effects. (Mirqāt)

The health risks that are associated with Shīsha are far more serious than cigarettes. Many Muslims and especially youngsters, regard it as a safe alternative to cigarettes and something pleasurable. An expert opinion of Dr. Mike Knapton, associate medical director at the BHF, is recorded in an article published in the T&A on 3rd March 2012. He said, "Contrary to popular belief, Shīsha is not safer than smoking cigarettes."

Change of Rulings with the Change of Circumstances
Some can argue that the previous Indian-subcontinent scholars issued a verdict that Shīsha is generally Makrūh-e-Tanzīhi (which merely means disliked but not unlawful). Many Fuqahā (jurists) like Allāmah Ibn Ābidīn As-Shāmi ﷽, have made it explicit that rulings and verdicts can vary due to the change of time and circumstances that are discussed by the classical scholars, in the books related to issuing verdicts. There are many examples in the books of Fiqh (Islamic jurisprudence) to be found, where the later scholars have issued verdicts contrary to previous scholars, due to the change of circumstances. Looking at the current climate and situation of the Muslims, in relation to Shīsha, it could be said with confidence, that if those same Indian-subcontinent scholars were to be alive today, saw the current situation of Shīsha bars and had became aware of the harmful effects of smoking Shīsha, they would most definitely give the verdict of it being totally unlawful.

Background on Shīsha (Water-Pipe Tobacco Smoking)
Shīsha is a water-pipe used to smoke a flavoured tobacco known as molasses. There are many common names given to water pipe

smoking, such as Hukkah, Argileh, Marghile, Shīsha and hubble-bubble. It first originated in ancient Persia and India. It was invented by an Indian physician during the reign of the Emperor Akbar called Hākim Abul-Fath, who suggested that tobacco should be first passed through a small receptacle of water so that it would be rendered harmless. However, this unsubstantiated belief subsequently became widespread, with the people of India and Persia thinking it to be less harmful. The water-pipe smoking eventually gained popularity and spread throughout the Middle East and Central Asia. It became widely used in places such as Turkey, Iran, Syria, Jordan, Lebanon and the Indian-subcontinent.

After the advent of the water-pipe tobacco smoking, in the late 20th century, supplementary products were introduced to add some flavourings to the tobacco, thus, combining tobacco with a sweetener (typically fruits). Unlike cigarettes, Shīsha is an exotic way of smoking tobacco in a fairly relaxed manner, in a social environment. It is available in many pre-packed quantities sold in a variety of flavours such as apple, banana, peach, cherry, coconut, orange, grape etc.

Description of the Usage of the Water-Pipe Smoking
A water-pipe mainly consists of four main parts:

- The head bowl where the tobacco is heated.
- A jar filled with water.
- A body/pipe which connects the head to the water bowl.

Contemporary Fiqh   Smoking Shīsha

- A hose and a mouth piece through which the smoke is inhaled by the smoker.

The tobacco that is placed on the head is moist and often sweetened with flavours. An aluminum foil with punctured holes, is then placed over the head to completely seal the tobacco. A charcoal is then lit (but does not burn in a self-sustained manner) and placed over the foil, on top of the tobacco filled head bowl (covered by perforated aluminum foil).

Once the head is loaded and the charcoal is lit, the smoker inhales the smoke through the hose and draws air through the body (connected to the head bowl and the water jar) and over the tobacco and charcoal. Having passed over the charcoal, the smoke (which now contains charcoal combustion products) passes through the tobacco and travels all the way down the water pipe body, bubbles through the water in the jar creating a vacuum of smoke above the water and finally, is carried through the hose into the smoker's mouth, with a mouthpiece. This process is repeated again and again, on average for 45-60 minutes by the smoker.

Health Effects According to Health Experts
Contrary to what Shīsha smokers commonly believe, Shīsha is associated with serious health risks. Amongst many health organisations, one of the world's leading health experts are the WHO (World Health Organisation. WHO is the directing and coordinating authority for health within the United Nations. It is responsible for providing leadership on global health matters, shaping the

health research agenda, setting norms and standards, articulating evidence-based policy options, providing technical support to countries and monitoring and assessing health trends.

Much research has been carried out by the WHO (World Health Organisation) and other organisations like ALA (American Lung Associations) and many empirical tests have also been carried out in laboratories, in establishing what health risks are involved in smoking Shīsha. The smoke that emits from the water-pipe contains high levels of toxic compounds including tar, carbon monoxide and heavy metals that causes lung cancer, heart disease, asthma attacks, emphysema and other serious illnesses. According to the WHO research, water-pipe tobacco smoking delivers the addictive nicotine drug and as in the case of cigarettes, more frequent use is associated with the smokers being more likely to report that they are addicted.

Furthermore, a water-pipe smoking session may expose the smoker to more smoke over a longer period of time than it occurs when smoking cigarettes. Cigarette smokers typically take 8-10 puffs, over 5-7 minutes and inhale 40-75 ml of smoke. In contrast, a water -pipe smoking session typically lasts 20-80 minutes during which, the smoker may take 50—200 puffs which range from about 0.15—1 litres of smoke. **The water-pipe smoker may therefore, inhale as much smoke during one session equivalent to a cigarette smoker inhaling from 100 - 200 cigarettes.**

What becomes clear from this is that smoking Shīsha is much more concentrated than smoking cigarettes. If cigarettes are known to cause severe health risks, then imagine what Shīsha is capable of. The exponents of Shīsha often argue that the toxic effect is filtered, when the tobacco smoke passes through water which therefore, reduces the risk to health. However, according to the WHO the water does not filter out the toxic ingredients because nicotine and tobacco smoke are not water-soluble. The smoke produced still contains high levels of toxic compounds including carbon monoxide, heavy metals and cancer-causing chemicals during inhalation. The WHO have gathered more facts about Shīsha smoking as follows:

1. Commonly used heat sources that are applied to burn the tobacco, such as charcoal, are more likely to increase health risks because when such fuels are combusted, they produce their own toxicants, including high levels of carbon monoxide.
2. Sharing a mouthpiece possesses a serious risk of transmission of disease, including tuberculosis and hepatitis. Water-pipe smoking is often sweetened and flavoured which makes it very appealing. The sweet smell and taste explains why some people, particularly young people are addicted to it .Thus, eventually, it increases the chances of serious health problems.
3. Shīsha smoke possesses dangers associated with second hand smoke.
4. Pregnant women and the foetus are particularly vulnerable when exposed either actively or involuntarily, to the water-pipe smoke toxicant which can result in low birth weight babies.

Social Harms According to the ALA (American Lung Association) Report

Previously, the common trend was to smoke Shīsha individually but today it is viewed as a social activity, often smoked by a group of people who share the same pipe and try different flavourings throughout the evening. Shīsha is perceived as a way to get together with friends and to have fun.

According to a research conducted by the ALA, the social aspect of water-pipe smoking may put many users at risk for other infectious disease such as tuberculosis and viruses such as hepatitis (inflammation of the liver causing fever, abdominal pain and weakness) and herpes (causing skin disease, painful blisters and inflammation). Shared mouthpieces and the heated moist smoke may enhance the opportunity for such diseases to spread.

Moreover, the second hand smoke from a water pipe is potentially dangerous because it contains smoke from tobacco itself, as well as the smoke from the heat source used to burn the tobacco. Likewise, being in an environment of overwhelming smoke for a long period causes severe dizziness and at times unconsciousness.

The Islamic Perspective

So far, we have looked at the harmful effects of Shīsha from a medical perspective. Now, I shall discuss the Islamic perspective of Shīsha.

1. The Body has Certain Rights Over Oneself

In Islām to safeguard ones body from harmful substances is obliga-

Contemporary Fiqh

Smoking Shīsha

tory. Everything in this world, including our body is the property of Allāh ﷻ. Allāh ﷻ states, **"To Him belongs all which is in the heavens and all that is in the earth and all that is between them and all that is under the soil."** (20:6)

Allāh ﷻ has dignified the human body and has endowed it to mankind in order to test whether mankind will utilise it in the right manner or not, or nourish it with lawful or unlawful consumptions. Allāh ﷻ states, **"The One Who created the heavens and the earth to test you, which one amongst you will do righteous deeds."** (67:2)

This sophisticated body is a wonderous miracle gifted by Allāh ﷻ. It is an example of one of the most complex 'machines' and a magnificent design by Allāh ﷻ. He states, **"Verily, We have created mankind in the best form."** (95:4)

Each organ functions uniquely and performs its duty dissimilarly to the other. Nevertheless, they all equally contribute in the preservation of the body. If one organ dysfunctions, then it will effect the entire body. So we can imagine how delicate our body is and how important it is to nourish it in the proper manner. It is thus, prohibited to nourish it with unlawful substances, or that which is detrimental for the body because it violates its sanctity. It is a well-known fact that whatever a person nourishes his body with, will surely have an impact on his behaviour and conduct.

Imām Bukhāri ﷺ relates in his Sahīh, the statement of Sayyidunā

Salmān Al-Fārsi ؓ when he once admonished Sayyidunā Abū Dardā ؓ, regarding his lengthy worships at night and perpetual fast throughout the days, "Verily your Lord has a right over you and your body has a right over you and your family has a right over you, so give each and everything the right it deserves." (Bukhāri)

In another narration, once the Holy Prophet ﷺ advised Sayyidunā Abdullāh Ibn Amr Ibnul-Ās ؓ, when he heard about his exaggeration in worship, "Your body has a right over you, your eyes have a right over you, your wife has a right over you." (Bukhāri, Muslim)

It is evident from the above Hadīth that Islām emphasises the maintenance of the body and fulfilling its rights. Unlawful or harmful consumption violates its basic right and its human sanctity.

2. Prohibition of Causing Harm to Ones Body
As was explained previously that in the Islamic perspective our body is the property of Allāh ﷻ, endowed to us by Him as a test. The body must be utilised and cherished in the way Allāh ﷻ has instructed us to do so. It is prohibited to deliberately cause harm to the body as Allāh ﷻ states in the Holy Qur'ān, **"And do not cast yourself into destruction with your own hands." (2:195)**

Although this command was revealed regarding a particular incident, nevertheless, the general implication of this verse is to abstain from that which is intended to harm ones body unnecessarily that which will eventually lead him towards destruction in this world and the Hereafter. Smoking Shīsha causes physical harm to ones body in this world and makes him accountable in the Hereafter for violating its sanctity.

Imām Hākim ﷺ and Imām Baihaqi ﷺ relate a Hadīth narrated by Sayyidunā Abū Saeed Al-Khudhri ؓ that the Holy Prophet ﷺ said, "There is no endurance of harm nor inflicting harm to anyone." In this Hadīth, the Holy Prophet ﷺ has forbidden inflicting harm upon ones self in any way and likewise, inflicting harm to someone else.

The Fuqahā (Muslim jurists) have deduced from this Hadīth a ruling of:

$$ الضَّرَرُ يُزَالُ $$

"Harmful things should be averted." (Al-Ashbāh wan Nadhā'ir)

This principle instructs to abandon and forsake those substances that directly cause harm to the body and without a doubt, smoking Shīsha is one of them.

3. More Harm to the Body than Benefit

Shīsha may have some questionable benefits, such as relaxation of tension. If this is the case, then the same argument can be made to justify alcohol, as some people drink to ease their tension, yet no Muslim will ever accept it. Its harm out-weighs its benefit.

Although it can be argued regarding its benefits, its harm out-weighs them as Allāh ﷻ states regarding alcohol, **"They ask you (O Muhammad) regarding alcohol and gambling, say within them there is great sin and (also) benefits for mankind, however, their sins are far greater than their benefits."** (2:219)

Allāh ﷻ outlines in the above verse, the nature of gambling and alcohol. Although some benefits are attainable from them, their harmful effects are much more severe than their benefits. The Fuqahā of this Ummah have derived the following principle from this verse. Imām Ibn Nujaym ﷭ writes:

$$درأ المفاسد اولیٰ من جلب المصالح$$

"To avert the harmful effects is more important than to attain the benefits." (Al-Ashbāh wan Nadhā'ir)

The fundamental principle to be understood here is that any substance in which its harmful effects outweigh its benefits, must not be used at all. It becomes necessary to abstain from it at all cost. Shīsha, undoubtedly, consists of more harms than benefit therefore, it must be avoided.

4. Blocking the Means
Another juristic principle that relates to Shīsha is "blocking the means" i.e. to abstain from those acts that lead towards other evils. For example, to cast ones gaze upon Ghair-Mahram (strange) women, eventually can lead to inclination towards fornication, therefore, to gaze at such women is prohibited. Islām takes preventive measures rather than suffering the consequences.

Shīsha opens the doors to other evils such as excessive pleasure, waste of time, extravagance, addiction, harming oneself progressively and free intermingling with the opposite gender.

Some may argue that smoking Shīsha once every so often cannot kill you nor put your health at risk. In that case, the same argument can be used with alcohol because the reason for its prohibition is it leads towards intoxication and many other evil acts; having one or two sips will surely not intoxicate anyone yet, the Shari'ah has still prohibited it for this reason.

Similarly, Shīsha contains the drug nicotine that causes addiction. Once a person becomes addicted to it, he is putting his health at serious risk. For this reason, the principle of blocking the means to prevent further evils is applicable to smoking Shīsha as well.

5. Slow Form of Suicide
Taking into consideration all of the above facts, smoking Shīsha can lead to eventual lung cancer, heart disease and many other serious illnesses which cause death. So the health risks associated with Shīsha eventually lead to death, whereby, the smoker becomes guilty of committing suicide but in a slow and gradual way. Allāh ﷻ says, **"And do not kill yourselves, verily, Allāh is very compassionate towards you." (4:29)**

Apart from the above, there are other contributing factors that make the smoking of Shīsha a serious issue:

A) Extravagance in Wealth

To spend money on that which by nature is not beneficial or excessive amount of unnecessary expenditure that is beyond ones needs or that which is directly instrumental for causing harm to the body are all forms of squandering wealth.

Allāh ﷻ has prohibited squandering ones wealth. Allāh ﷻ states in the Holy Qur'ān, **"And do not squander (your wealth). Indeed the squanderers are the brothers of Shaytān." (17:27)**
In another verse of the Holy Qur'ān Allāh ﷻ states, **"And do not waste, for Allāh does not love those who waste." (6:141)**

The Holy Prophet ﷺ forbade the squandering of wealth in the following Hadīth, "Verily Allāh ﷻ has prohibited for you disobedience to parents, burying daughters alive, to deny what you owe and demand what you have no right to and He has disliked for you hearsay (gossip), excessive questioning and the squandering of wealth." (Bukhāri, Muslim)

The smoking of Shīsha is squandering ones wealth, so in this aspect, it can also be ruled as prohibited.

B) Emitting Unpleasant Smell from the Mouth

The Holy Prophet ﷺ prevented people from entering the Masjid, or coming in contact with anyone, if they had eaten raw garlic and onions due to the bad odour the mouth emitted.
The Holy Prophet ﷺ said, "Whoever eats (raw) garlic or onion should keep away from us, keep far away from our Masājid and should sit at home."

This was so that the Musallis (those performing Salāh in the Masjid) and other people are not harmed because of the bad odour. This was the command about something that is generally permissible to consume, so imagine how much more severe it would be to smoke Shīsha, which in itself is very harmful. Although it may consist of flavouring, the purpose is to encourage someone to smoke excessively. Thus, the tobacco effect still remains in the mouth and on the body which eventually emits an unpleasant smell.

The Opening of Shīsha Bars

There has been an increase in the number of Shīsha bars in many parts of the UK. Unlike cigarettes, smoking Shīsha is generally perceived as a social practice. This inevitably brings about more negative effects socially, morally and spiritually that many Muslims are unaware of. As discussed earlier, Islām takes preventive measures rather than suffering the consequences, by imposing those rules that block the means. Some of the negative effects that Shīsha bars bring about are as follows:

1. Negative Social Impact - Free Mixing and Informal Interaction of Both Genders

In the UK, as well as around the world, there is an increase in immorality such as fornication, adultery, illegitimate babies, rape, cheating on ones spouse, resulting in family breakdown and so on. One of the main contributing factors of such acts is not controlling the gaze and free intermingling of both genders. Islām is not merely a religion that admonishes, but rather, it is a practical religion, providing solutions to prevent immorality. Modern society views intermingling of both genders as progression of mankind, whereas, in reality, this has drastically degenerated the dignity of mankind. The increase of rape, fornication, abortion, illegitimate relationships, cheating on one another etc. bear testimony to this. This is why Islām is emphatic on implementing a system of segregation between both genders and the idea is not to degrade women but rather, to enforce morality within the society, dispel immoral behaviour and preserve the chastity and dignity of women.

Once an Ottoman scholar, Ahmad Wafīq Pāsha, replied to a question posed to him, at a congress in Europe as to why Eastern women remain in the confinements of their houses and do not freely mingle with men. His immediate reply was, "Because our women do not desire to become pregnant except with their husbands."

It is very unfortunate that in the current climate we are living in today, many of our Muslim brothers and sisters are ensnared in illegitimate relationships and other immoral behaviour. All this is due to free social interaction of both genders.

Almost every Shīsha bar promotes the free mixing of both genders. They are a means of invitation towards sins and other immoral acts. Many Muslim brothers go to Shīsha bars specifically to mingle with other women and cast unlawful gazes upon them whilst many Muslim sisters dress to impress men, immerse themselves in excessive fragrance and wear glamorous and attractive clothing. In this way, they are directly or indirectly luring men. So both will receive a share of the sin.

In a Hadīth of Sahīh Muslim, it is narrated that the Holy Prophet ﷺ prohibited women to immerse themselves in fragrance when attending the congregational prayer in the Masjid. This is how much emphasis Islām gives in regards to setting limits in dressing when emerging from the home.

Allāh ﷻ, through His Divine Wisdom, knows what is harmful for us and what leads one to destruction, so He has instructed men and women to lower their gazes and prohibited free mixing in order to attain purity.

Allāh ﷻ states, **"Say to the believing men to lower their gaze and safeguard their private parts; this is more pure for them, verily, Allāh is All-Aware of what they do. And say to the believing women to lower their gaze and safeguard their private parts." (24:30- 31)**

"He knows the fraud of the eyes and what the hearts conceal." (40:19)

Sayyidunā Abū Usayd ؓ relates that he heard the Holy Prophet ﷺ addressing (the women), upon seeing men and women mixing after emerging from the Masjid, "Draw back because you have no right to walk in the middle of the path (i.e. to walk with men) but keep to the side of the road. Thereafter, the women kept so close to the wall (and away from men) that their garments were rubbing against it." (Abū Dāwūd)

Contemporary Fiqh   Smoking Shīsha

This Hadīth forbids the free mixing of men and women, even if it is outside the Masjid, in spite of it being one of the greatest symbols of Islām. Therefore, any Shīsha bar that provides free mixed facilities are not only sinful but in actual fact, opening the doors towards immorality.

2. Music, Singing and Dancing

Apart from promoting informal interaction between both genders, many Shīsha bars consist of loud music and some even consist of singing and dancing. This poses a serious threat to Muslims, spiritually, physically, psychologically and emotionally. Music causes arousal in a person and arouses him to commit sin because much music carries a general theme of love, emotion, fornication, crime and romance. This greatly influences emotion and psychological behaviour.

As mentioned previously, Islām adopts preventive measures and blocks the means that lead to other sins. Many severe warnings have been mentioned with regards to music, singing and dancing:

a) Allāh ﷻ says, **"And there are among men, those that purchase idle tales, to mislead (men) from the path of Allāh and throw ridicule. For such there will be a humiliating punishment."** (31:6)

Sayyidunā Abdullāh Ibn Mas'ūd ﷺ states in the explanation of the word "idle tales", that it refers to singing. (Tafseer Ibn Kathīr)
Hasan Al-Basri ﷺ says, "This verse was revealed in relation to singing and musical instruments." (Tafsīr Ibn Kathīr)

b) Sayyidunā Abū Mālik Al-Ash'ari ؓ reports that he heard the Holy Prophet ﷺ say, "There will appear some people in my Ummah, who will hold adultery, silk, alcohol and musical instruments to be lawful." (Bukhāri)

c) Sayyidunā Imrān Ibn Husain ؓ reports that the Holy Prophet ﷺ said, "This Ummah will experience the swallowing up of some people by the earth, formation of some people into animals and stones being rained upon them."

A man from amongst the Muslims asked, "O Messenger of Allāh ﷺ! When will this be?" The Holy Prophet ﷺ replied, "When female singers and musical instruments appear and alcohol will become (widely) consumed." (Tirmizi, Ibn Mājah)

d) Sayyidunā Ali ؓ reports that the Holy Prophet ﷺ said, "When my Ummah begin doing fifteen things, they will be inflicted with tribulations... and (from those 15 things he said) when female singers and musical instruments become widespread." (Tirmizi)

What is the Islamic Ruling of those People's Income Who Provide Water-pipe Smoking (Shīsha)

Another Islamic ruling that transpires from this is the income of those that sell or provide Shīsha. Shaykh Khālid Saifullāh Rahmāni, one of the renowned scholars, states that the general principle of buying and selling in Islām is that any merchandise that itself is lawful, would be permissible to sell, that which is unlawful (Harām) would be Harām to sell and that which is Makrūh

Contemporary Fiqh   Smoking Shīsha

would be Makrūh to sell. (Kitābul Fatāwa)

Since we have presented sufficient evidence and their reasons to prove that water-pipe smoking and opening Shīsha bars is unlawful and prohibited, the source of income derived from buying/ selling water-pipes, smoking and opening Shīsha bars, will fall under the category of unlawful.

Conclusion

By now, it has become apparent that smoking Shīsha is associated with many serious harmful effects medically, physically and spiritually. Shīsha cannot be classed as Makrūh-e-Tanzīhi (which merely implies to a disliked act and no sin). Smoking Shīsha infringes many of the Islamic laws which renders it to be unlawful. Furthermore, the Shīsha bars that currently operate today consist of many unlawful activities and pose a serious threat to the Muslim community. What goes on behind the scenes in many of these bars makes them no different to pubs, with the exception that alcohol is not served. Due to the severity of the crime, the Fatwa in our time in regards to Shīsha is Harām or at least Makrūh-e-Tahrīmi as both terms imply it to be unlawful and a sinful act. In addition, the income received in providing it or opening Shīsha bars cannot be classed as Halāl income.

Allāh ﷻ Knows Best

Planning for a Baby
Dr Rafaqat Rashid

Q Me and my husband are newly married and have been trying to have a baby for about 10 months now, with no luck. Is there any advice you can give us regarding increasing our chances?

A Firstly, I would like to say that this problem is not uncommon and that doctors would **not** normally refer a couple like yourselves for investigations until you had been trying to conceive regularly and frequently for at least a full year. Some medical tips to help conceive are as follows:

1. Ask your doctor or pharmacist for folic acid tablets 0.4mg to be taken daily prior to becoming pregnant and for the first 2-3 months as this will reduce the chance of your baby having neural tube defects (i.e. spina bifida) by approximately 70%.

2. It is important that you try to conceive regularly, on average twice a week, as this will increase your chances. The missionary position or 'natural position' has been shown to be more effective, where the wife is below the husband. When the wife is lying on her back it assists the sperm in reaching its destination. A thin pillow under the wife's hips is another good tip.

3. There is strong evidence to suggest that lying on your back for 10 minutes after intercourse increases chances of conceiving as it increases the odds of the male sperm meeting the female egg. Sometimes, couples immediately go to the bathroom to have a Ghusl. I would advise a short waiting period prior to Ghusl or

Wudhu, though Ghusl and Wudhu are virtuous acts and are recommended to gain Barakah (blessings).

4. Try to increase the frequency of intercourse approximately 5 days before the wife is likely to be ovulating (i.e. when she expels her female egg from her ovary into her fallopian tubes to be fertilised by her husband's sperm). This is the most fertile period and usually occurs between the female periods, mid-cycle. Make a note in your diary of your period times (i.e. number of days and when it starts). Ovulation typically occurs approximately 14 days (in a 28 day cycle) before the beginning of the next period. The wife's discharge usually becomes thicker and stickier during this phase.

5. Avoid vaginal sprays, scented tampons and lubricants as these can cause an imbalance of the vaginal PH and reduce the effectiveness of the sperm.

6. As Muslims, we should abstain from toxic substances such as smoking, drugs and alcohol. Besides being disliked in Islām, they are damaging to fertility. There is evidence to suggest regular and frequent caffeine can also reduce chances of conception as it restricts the blood flow to the womb. More than 3 cups of tea a day is excessive.

7. Be aware of any medication that you may be taking on prescription, or over the counter which may either reduce your chances of conception, or could be harmful to the baby if you conceive.

8. The husband should avoid tight underwear or trousers, saunas, and hot baths as this reduces sperm count.

Contemporary Fiqh — Planning a Baby

9. Stay active and healthy with exercise and a healthy balanced diet. Do not overdo the exercise as this can have the opposite affect, nor go onto extreme diets. These can effect ovulation and sperm function.

10. It is very important to try not to be stressed as this can cause issues for both husband and wife. Try not to be disheartened and not to be negative. Have Tawakkul (reliance) in Allāh ﷻ and turn to Him.

There are some remedies from the Holy Qur'ān related to this also by Shaykh Ashraf Ali Thānwi ﷫.

1. Read the following verse regularly in Arabic and make plenty of Du'ā to Allāh ﷻ.

وَلَوْ أَنَّ قُرْآنًا سُيِّرَتْ بِهِ الْجِبَالُ أَوْ قُطِّعَتْ بِهِ الْأَرْضُ أَوْ كُلِّمَ بِهِ الْمَوْتَىٰ بَلْ لِلَّهِ الْأَمْرُ جَمِيعًا

"And even if there was a Qur'ān with which mountains were moved, or earth was cloven asunder, or the dead are spoken to, (they would not believe), but truly the command is with Allāh in all things." (13:31)

2. Call Allāh ﷻ by the following Beautiful Names seven times every day after Iftār, whilst fasting for seven days:

"Ya Bāri (O' Evolver), Ya Musawwir (O' Fastener)"

If two weeks have passed since the wife has ovulated and her period has not begun as yet, then it would be worthwhile getting a reliable home pregnancy test. If the test is positive, it is very likely that she is pregnant and if the test is negative then it is likely that she is not pregnant, though it may be worthwhile testing again after 1-2 weeks. (If the test is done too soon, there will not be enough hCG in the urine to make the test positive). Remember that a period can be missed for many other reasons other than pregnancy, such as jet lag, severe illness, surgery, shock, bereavement or other causes of stress.

Allāh ﷻ Knows Best

Depression

Dr Rafaqat Rashid

Q **Dear Doctor Sāhib, I have been diagnosed with depression for over 8 months now and have recently been started on antidepressants. I feel very low in mood and it is affecting my Imān. Should I continue with my medication and what other advice would you give me?**

A I have seen and treated many cases of Muslim patients who have reached the pits with their Imān because of their uncontrollable depression. However, having treated them medically, they have become strong enough to work and strengthen their Imān again and have successfully overcome their depression. Depressive disorders make you feel exhausted, worthless, helpless, and hopeless. Such negative thoughts and feelings make some people feel like giving up, which will have a serious effect on their Imān. You should realise that these negative views are part of depression and typically do not accurately reflect your life situation or your negligence of Islām and Allāh ﷻ. Negative thinking fades as treatment begins to take effect.

When I see Muslim patients who are suffering with depression and are truly seeking help, then I usually give them the following practical advice:

- Do not set difficult goals for yourself or take on additional responsibility.
- Break large tasks into small ones, set some priorities and do

Contemporary Fiqh · Depression

what you can as you can.

- Do not expect too much from yourself too soon, as this will only increase your feelings of failure.
- Try to be with other people (especially religious people who are positive in their approach); it is better than being alone or being with sinful people.
- Force yourself to participate in activities that may make you feel better, especially those activities that you enjoy doing and are pleasing to Allāh ﷻ.
- Try participating in religiously orientated social activities.
- Do not overdo it or get upset if your mood is not greatly improved right away. Feeling better takes time. Just because you are not coping too well does not mean that you are less religious than those who cope well. Many environmental factors play a role in how you react to stress not just religious ones. The idea is to strive towards overcoming worldly stressors.
- Do not make major life decisions, such as changing jobs, getting married or divorced, without consulting others who know you well and who have a more objective view of your situation. In any case, it is advisable to postpone important decisions until your depression has lifted.
- Do not expect to snap out of your depression. People rarely do. Help yourself as much as you can and do not blame yourself for not being up to par. Have trust in Allāh ﷻ for He will respond to your prayers.
- Remember, do not accept your negative thinking. It is part of the depression and will disappear as your depression

responds to treatment.

- Get help from a professional if your symptoms seem to get progressively worse. No matter how much you want to beat it yourself, you may find that your low mood is better having talked to a doctor or other health professional. After all, clinical depression is classified as a medical illness in these circumstances because it now has physical manifestations.

Depression is a very common condition today. Unfortunately, because of the social problems that Muslims are faced with in today's society, some depressive patients may have uncontrollable symptoms. These patients should seek medical help but should always have trust in Allāh ﷻ.

To have complete Tawakkul (trust) in Allāh ﷻ means to rely on Him completely and to recognise that ones life and destiny is totally owned and controlled by Him. If Allāh ﷻ wishes, He may use medical help as a means of controlling your depression and this should not be considered a wrong thing but a positive thing, as the person is trying to get back to sanity so that they can cope with life and overcome those hindrances that are holding back their Imān. It is important to understand that seeking help in times of despair is something that Allāh ﷻ expects from us for we are His mere creations, **"Truly no one despairs of God's Soothing Mercy, except those who have no faith." (12:87)**

Allāh ﷻ Knows Best

Chronic Depression
Dr Rafaqat Rashid

Q I feel very depressed and have been like this for years. I have tried doctors and counsellors but they do not work and I do not want to take depression tablets. Please can you give me some advice on how I should carry on?

A It seems you have chronic depression and my advice to you is to ponder on and implement the following Islamic advice into your life:

The truth is that we have been created by Allāh ﷻ to be tested and tried. **"Every soul shall have a taste of death and We test you by evil and by good by way of trial. To Us must you return."** (21:35)

This trial is conducted through the difficult situations we are exposed to. If we are put through good and pleasant circumstances, then our trial is about whether we remain thankful to Allāh ﷻ. If we are put through bad or stressful circumstances, then our trial is whether or not we show perseverance and patience in these times. Allāh ﷻ tests us through hardships for a number of reasons:

1. To teach us a lesson for our own misdoings: **"Whatever misfortune happens to you, is because of the things your hands have brought and for many (sins) He grants forgiveness."** (42:30)

2. To see whether we are truly grateful to our Lord at all times: **"Now, as for man, when his Lord tries him, giving him honour and gifts, then says he, (puffed up), 'My Lord has honoured me'. But when He tries him, restricting his sustenance for him, then says he (in despair), 'My Lord has humiliated me.'" (89:15-16)**

3. To clean the evil within us: **"Allāh will not leave the believers in the state in which you are now, until He separates what is evil from what is good". (3:179)**

4. To give us the opportunity to earn reward by showing patience: **"And because they were patient and constant, He will reward them with a garden and (garments of) silk." (76:12)**

Islām has been teaching us the psychology of coping since the time of the Holy Prophet 🌸. It is our loss that we have not used this in our daily lives effectively. Islām teaches us that it is the attitude of the individual, to the stressful situation, that has a large impact on how positively that individual responds. This attitude is a learned experience which one adheres to at all times, especially at the time of need. Islām provides the essential ingredients to remedy all daunting situations. The following are a few examples:

1. Work towards increasing your Imān by increasing the performance of righteous deeds.

"Whoever works righteousness, male or female, and has faith,

verily, to him We will give a good life that is good and pure and We shall pay them certainly, a reward in proportion to the best of what they used to do." (16:97)

Lots of benefits are gained through this. The person becomes resilient, his willpower becomes stronger, He becomes more patient, the hope of reward is further increased and thus, his anxiety may even be replaced with an inner joy.

2. Always acknowledge and be aware that any distress and worry in this life earns expiation for your sins, purifies your heart and raises your status.

The Holy Prophet ﷺ said, "No illness, fatigue, sickness or grief befalls the Muslim, not even worries, but it will be an expiation for some of his sins." (Muslim)

3. Constantly remind yourself about the reality of this world. This world is a temporary abode for us. We are drowned in its luxuries yet we fail to gain constant happiness.

Life is apparently unjust in this world and to expect perfection and happiness throughout life is a deception. The true abode is the hereafter and this life is just a testing ground for us, yet we live in this life and become so engrossed with the most pettiest of things as if our whole life depended on it.

Life is about ups and downs. A bit of laughter one day and many tears the next. It is how we persevere through this, which is im-

Contemporary Fiqh   Chronic Depression

portant. The believer is only detained here, as the Holy Prophet ﷺ said, "This world is a prison for the believer and paradise for the non-believer." (Muslim)

4. Always refer to the lives and examples of Prophets of Allāh ﷻ and the pious. The Prophets of Allāh ﷻ and the pious undoubtedly, suffered more distress in this world than any other people. Each person is tested according to his strength. One thing is for sure that when Allāh ﷻ takes a liking to a person, He tests him.

"No burden do We place on any soul, but that which it can bear." (6:152)

Sayyidunā Sa'd ؓ asked the Holy Prophet ﷺ, "O Messenger of Allāh ﷻ, which of the people suffers the most distress?" He said: "The Prophets, then those who come after them (in terms of status), then those who come after them. A man will be tested according to the strength of his faith. If his faith is strong, then the distress with which he is tried will be greater; if his faith is weak, he will be tested in accordance with the level of his faith. Distress will keep on befalling the slave until he walks on the face of the earth free from sin." (Bukhāri)

5. Always focus on the Hereafter and make this the utmost priority of your main concern. It was narrated by Sayyidunā Anas Ibn Mālik ؓ that the Holy Prophet ﷺ said, "Whoever is mainly concerned about the Hereafter, Allāh ﷻ will make him feel independent of others and will make him focused and content, and his worldly affairs will fall into place. However, whoever is mainly

Concerned with this world, Allāh ﷻ will make him feel in constant need of others and will make him distracted and unfocused, and he will get nothing of this world except what is decreed for him." (Tirmizi)

6. Remember death and that every living thing will meet its Maker. This world is only temporary and the real life is the one hereafter. For a believer, the greatest comfort is that the stresses of this world are only limited to this world and appreciating the temporariness of this life eases the burden for him.

The Holy Prophet ﷺ said, "Remember frequently the one who will destroy all your pleasures: death, for there is no-one who remembers death when in straitened circumstances, but his situation will become easier, and there is no-one who remembers death during times of ease, but his circumstances will become straitened."

(Muslim)

7. Increase your supplication to Allāh ﷻ and seek His help. Du'ā (prayer or supplication) is the essence of worship and includes both protection and treatment. Allāh ﷻ has full control of all matters and it is only Him who can change things in this world, according to how He wishes. This is why the Prophets ﷺ turned towards Allāh ﷻ and prayed to Him for refuge from distress frequently.

Sayyidunā Yaqūb ﷺ said, **"I complain of my sorrow and grief only to Allāh." (12:86)**

Contemporary Fiqh / Chronic Depression

"When My servants ask you concerning Me, I am indeed close (to them); I listen to the prayer of every supplicant when he calls on Me; let them also, with a will, listen to My call and believe in Me; that they may walk in the right way." (2:186)

8. Send abundant salutations on our beloved Prophet ﷺ. This is one of the greatest ways through which Allāh ﷻ may relieve worries. Sayyidunā Tufayl Ibn Ubayy Ibn Ka'b ؓ reported that his father said to the Holy Prophet ﷺ, "I will devote all my prayers (salutations) to you." The Holy Prophet ﷺ replied, "Then your worries will be taken care of and your sins will be forgiven."

9. Rely upon Allāh ﷻ and trust Him with all matters. **"And whosoever puts his trust in Allāh, then He will suffice him." (65:3)**

10. Think about what matters today in a positive way. Do not worry about what may happen tomorrow or regret what happened yesterday.

Allāh ﷻ Knows Best

Autism

Dr Rafaqat Rashid

Q Dear Doctor, I have a 7 year old nephew who the doctors have said is autistic. I am worried that my 4 year old son might be autistic because he behaves in a similar way. How do I find out and what should I do?

A There is no simple way to answer your question except to explain what Autism is and what its symptoms are. Autism is a disorder that falls into a group of disorders called the Autistic Spectrum Disorders (ASD). 1 in 100 people have ASD in the UK. The disorder is life-long and can affect a child's ability to communicate well with others or to play and socialise. This disorder can affect children in many different ways and so, is termed a spectrum disorder. It can present as moderate to serious learning disabilities to minor difficulties in the child's ability to socialise. The spectrum disorder can vary to the extent that some children with the condition exhibit obvious learning problems or odd behaviour in school, whilst others are quite bright or gifted in their academic abilities, yet may find it difficult to socialise and so prefer to play alone.

An ASD child's behaviour can sometimes be mistaken as deliberate misbehaviour and so they may be labelled as naughty with little interest in learning. This can be very troublesome when the teachers at school might not be experienced in identifying traits of ASD in children or when they go to the evening classes (Makhtab) and the teachers may find the child disruptive, inattentive or arrogant.

Early Signs:
If your child exhibits some of the following symptoms, it does not necessarily mean he or she has ASD. The diagnosis is not always as simple as that and can take a few years for the health professionals to decide. Some children may not have these obvious symptoms yet they may be considered as having ASD. These symptoms are just a guide. If you feel your child has some of these symptoms and they are obvious, not just traits, then you should seek advice from your health visitor, school nurse or GP. It is usually the paediatrician or child psychologist, who will decide on a diagnosis.

- Not babbling, pointing, or making meaningful gestures by 1 year of age
- Not speaking one word by 16 months
- Not combining two words by 2 years
- Not responding to his/her name
- Poor language or social skills
- Has difficulty interpreting what others are thinking or feeling.
- Has poor eye contact
- Has repetitive movements such as rocking or twirling, or self-abusive behaviour such as head-banging.
- Does not seem to know how to play with toys
- Excessively lines up toys or other objects
- Is attached to one particular toy or object
- Does not smile
- Has low or high sensitivity to pain, noise, light or crowds.

Problems ASD Children Encounter:

1) Problems Socialising - ASD children may have difficulty in reading body language and facial expressions and therefore, can sometimes misunderstand non-verbal cues. They may also take words literally and become confused with normal daily verbal expressions like, "'you need to pull up your socks and work harder!'" They are likely to take this literally and may literally pull up their socks. They can have difficulty understanding others' feelings or emotions. This can all contribute to significant deficiencies in the art of communication, which we take for granted. They may seem untactful and insensitive in conversation. They may find it difficult to make friends or seem unusual to others in conversation or even in bodily expressions, preferring their own company rather than the company of others. New places and situations may make them quite anxious as it may be very confusing for them to interact with something they have not been exposed to before. They can find it more difficult to adapt. These symptoms vary considerably with each child and the intensity can also vary in different ASD children.

2) Work Around Routines

ASD children do not like change as it can be very confusing for them to approach new situations that go against their normal daily routine. For this reason, they may become anxious and irritable if things are not according to how they expected them to be. Their capacity to adapt to new situations may be good if they are prepared; it is rather the unpredictability that bothers them the most. They may seem to have unusual behaviour such as placing their clothes in a certain order, or they may be very particular about how things are done, in the order in which they are done and who does them. It may take a mother of an ASD child an hour or more to put him to sleep because of his nightly ritual routines.

3) Varied Sensitivity of Senses

The senses of ASD children may be over-sensitive or under-sensitive. This can affect any of the 5 senses. They may be very sensitive to certain colours/light, noises, smells, touch and tastes. They may be particular about food or certain smells may make them very irritable and anxious. Certain clothes may cause them anguish and so they may be particular about the clothes they wear because of the feel of the material. They may not like to be touched and cuddled. They may be under-sensitive and not perceive pain or temperature as would others. The reduced bodily awareness may make it difficult for them to balance well and they may present as clumsy.

4) Learning and Interest Issues

Some ASD children may have difficulties in learning and so may struggle at school or Makhtab (evening classes). They may be more demanding and require more attention. Some ASD children may be very bright with above average intelligence but have difficulties with socialising. Many ASD children have intense interests in certain hobbies or activities and can be very creative. They may become 'whiz kids' with computers as there is a rather predictable pattern to the workings of such an activity which is stimulating for such a child. Children with ASD can vary considerably.

Autism is not a very talked about subject in South Asian families yet it has a significant prevalence. There may be many cases of undiagnosed children who are just considered as anti-social and badly behaved. These children lose out on that extra attention that diagnosed ASD children may get from schools. It can sometimes be a taboo subject to admit that one has a child with ASD for the fear of how family and friends may react towards the parents or the child.

The solution is, if in doubt, seek help and advice from the school nurse, GP or health visitor.

Allāh ﷻ Knows Best

Sleeping Problems
Dr Rafaqat Rashid

Q Dear Doctor Sāhib, I have been having poor sleep now for over a month and my sleep is not getting any better. My doctor is not giving me any sleeping tablets and I am fed up because it makes me very tired in the day and I have 3 young children to take care of. Can you give me some advice? What should I do to help me with my sleep?

A Sleep is truly a blessing from Allāh ﷻ. Problems with sleep are quite common and are usually due to many reasons. Your question is quite brief, so it will not be possible for me to give you specific advice about your situation. I will attempt to explain sleeping problems generally, their causes and their remedies and hopefully you might be able to relate to this and benefit and at the same time readers can also benefit. Before I begin, I will just point out that lack of sleep is termed 'insomnia'.

Causes of Insomnia
Physical Causes - Symptoms such as pain, fever, irritability due to an acute illness (e.g. flu), injury and chronic illness, (such as arthritis) or hormonal states (such as menstruation/pregnancy/menopause) can be possible causes that can lead to insomnia. A patient is usually able to identify these physical causes for their insomnia.

Psychological Causes - These are not as easily identifiable as there are many psychological states that can potentially cause insomnia.

Stress due to work/family, depression, bereavement, jet lag or even excitement!

Induced Causes - These are not always identified causes and sometimes require advice from a health professional. Certain pre-scribed medication may cause problems with sleep and recreational/social drugs or stimulants such as caffeine/nicotine/alcohol etc. The sleep environment can also affect sleep, such as extremes of cold, a snoring partner, an uncomfortable bed, sleeping on a full stomach, too much vigorous activity before bed or shift work.

Idiopathic - When no obvious cause is ascertained and the insomnia is chronic, then at times family history of insomnia is sometimes seen as a possible cause in about 35% of chronic insomnia patients.

When Does Insomnia Become Serious

Lack of sleep is a cause for concern when you begin to have a number of the following symptoms. You should then seek professional help if these symptoms uncontrollably persist:

- Feeling tired, drowsy and irritable during the day.
- Poor concentration and diminishing performance during the day at work, school etc.
- Less alert and slowed down, delayed responses (can put a person at risk when driving).
- Regular colds/flu because of a weakened immune system.
- Symptoms of anxiety, depression and substance abuse.

Treatment of Insomnia

Once the cause of the insomnia is found, it should be treated and its symptoms relieved. For example, strong painkillers at night for pain, treatment for stress, anxiety and depression and abstaining from those things that induce poor sleep etc. If, however the cause is either not found or is difficult to fully eliminate, then you can use some of the following methods:

1. Sleeping Tips

- Have a fixed time of going to sleep and waking and follow the same routine always.
- Do not just lie in bed reading or talking to a partner, rather use it for sleeping purposes only. If you are not able to sleep in 15 to 20 minutes go into another room and do a light activity like reading the Holy Qur'ān.
- Avoid naps in the day and late meals (at least 4-5 hours before going to sleep) and excessive exercise before bed.
- Avoid caffeine, excessive fluids before bed. Take a hot bath but not within 2 hours of going to bed as this will have the opposite effect.
- Relax for half an hour before going to bed and do not focus on the time. A good activity before bed is to read the Holy Qur'ān as this will wind you down and relax you.
- Eating well with regular daily exercise will help you to remain fit. By being inactive and unhealthy, tiredness at night is less likely to occur.
- Relaxation exercises before going to sleep can be helpful such as Progressive Muscle Relaxation (PMR) - "Lie down or make

Contemporary Fiqh · Sleeping Problems

yourself comfortable. Starting at your toes, tense all the muscles as tightly as you can. Then, after tensing, completely relax your muscles. Continue to do this for every muscle group in your body, working your way up from your feet to the top of your head."(Saisan, J)

2. A Suggested Spiritual Approach

If one is lying in bed and is unable to sleep after 15 to 20 minutes, perform Wudhu (ablution) and go into another room and slowly recite Sūrah Mujādalah (Sūrah 58). (Remedies from the Holy Qur'ān)

Making Duā' is only truly effective if done with conviction. One must believe that Allāh ﷻ will resolve sleeping difficulties. One must be positive that his sleep will improve and not to be anxious about it. A recommended Du'ā is as follows:

اَللّٰهُمَّ غَارَتِ النُّجُوْمُ، وَهَدَأَتِ الْعُيُوْنُ، وَأَنْتَ حَيٌّ قَيُّوْمٌ، لَا تَأْخُذُكَ سِنَةٌ وَلَا نَوْمٌ، يَا حَيُّ يَا قَيُّوْمُ، أَهْدِئُ لَيْلِيْ، وَأَنِمْ عَيْنِيْ

Allāhumma Ghāratin-nujūmu wa hada'atil-uyūnu wa anta Hayyun Qayyūmun lā ta'khuzuka sinatuw-wa lā naumun yā Hayyu yā Qayyūmu ahdi' layli wa anim ayni.

"O Allāh, the stars have sunk and the eyes have turned tranquil and You are eternally Alive, the Self-Sustaining Sustainer of all. You do not slumber nor sleep overtakes You. Yā Hayyu! Yā Qayyūm! Grant me rest tonight and let my eyes sleep." (Hisnul

Haseen - Radiant Prayers by Mufti Muhammad Taqi Uthmāni)

Then, return to bed using the following relaxation technique. Perform Wudhu and then sleep on ones right side with the right hand under the right cheek. Once relaxed, close the eyes and take deep, slow breaths, making each breath even deeper than the last. Breathe in through your nose and out through your mouth. You can try making each exhale a little longer than each inhale. Concentrate on how relaxed this is making you. Picture the Ka'bah in your mind with all its tranquillity and quietness around it and focus on your breathing by gently saying, "Allāh ﷻ" as you exhale, yet at the same time thinking of Allāh's ﷻ Glory and Might. Slowly prolonging the word "Allāh ﷻ" as one exhales slowly. Hopefully, this will relax you to sleep, Inshā-Allāh.

Herbal Supplements.
These can be used but there is no valid evidence that they work effectively to improve sleep. Some examples are; chamomile, valerian root, kava kava, lemon balm, passionflower, lavender, and St. John's Wort. One must also remember that just because something is herbal, does not mean that they do not have side effects or that they may not interact with other medication. St John's Wort is probably the most recommended of the herbal therapies.

Prescribed Medication
There are different types of sleeping tablets but generally, they should always be used as a last resort, mainly because most sleeping tablets have a tendency to addiction if misused. Sometimes, patients are advised by their GP not to take them every night but a

Contemporary Fiqh   Sleeping Problems

few times a week. If taken for a while, they should be withdrawn gradually because of rebound insomnia after stopping them. This should be discussed with the health professional.

Q I would like you to give me some advice on ways to help me sleep. I have had this problem for over a year now. I have tried everything but nothing works. Even sleeping tablets do not work.

A What you are describing is what is termed as 'insomnia'. Insomnia refers to the disturbance of a normal sleep pattern. Sleep is an essential part of our life cycle as it allows us time to rest our mind and body, building our strength for what we are to be exposed to in the day. If it was not for sleep, our bodies and mind would not be able to bear the challenges and tasks we are expected to undertake during the rest of the day or night. Sleep maintains and preserves our emotional, psychological and physical states. Our emotional, psychological and physical states are an important part of our functioning and survival. Thus, it is Allāh's ﷻ grace upon mankind that He bestows us this blessing in order to preserve them.

"And among His signs are your sleep by night and day and your search for His grace (livelihood). Verily in that are signs for those who comprehend." [30:23]

Sleep protects us from the exhaustions of worldly affairs. Night is like a veil or cover which summons us to sleep, so that we may rest and then prepare for the coming day. It is a means of revival and rejuvenation.

"And He made the night a covering for you, and sleep a rest; and He made the day a means of revival." [25:47]

Allāh's ﷻ grace and blessings are only truly appreciated by us when they are taken away. Then, we understand the worth of such blessings and the mercy of Allāh ﷻ on His creation. Ask those who struggle with sleeping, how much they value it!

Stages of Sleep and Types of Insomnia
When we are asleep, our body experiences 3 stages of rest, each lasting approximately 90 minutes:

(1) Light sleep
(2) Deep sleep
(3) Rapid eye movement (REM) sleep

If these three stages are disturbed over a prolonged period, our health can be seriously affected. This can then hinder our general, intellectual and physical functioning and affect us psychologically by causing irritability, mental exhaustion and emotional vulnerability. Insomnia can last for days, months or even years and is therefore classified as:

- Transient insomnia (2-3 days).
- Short-term insomnia (few days to less than three weeks).
- Chronic insomnia (most nights for three weeks or more)

It is the chronic insomnia which can lead to mental health problems, such as anxiety and depression and physical problems, such as high blood pressure and obesity, which in turn can increase our risks of heart disease and diabetes etc.

Nearly everyone has problems sleeping at some time. It is estimated that approximately a third of the UK population has a period of insomnia at any one time.

Causes of Insomnia

Insomnia is caused by a number of factors:

1. Biological - Withdrawal from medicines, alcohol and other such medications. Pain and other physical distress such as coughing, breathlessness, stomach ulcers and excessive itching.

2. Environmental - Disrupted environment such as noise (snoring etc.), excessive light or extreme temperature, jet lag, shift work.

3. Psychological - Emotional distress and anxiety (bereavement, relationship problems, financial stress, mental health problems such as depression, dementia or psychosis etc.).

Spiritual Treatment

The most common cause of insomnia is anxiety, worry and any form of stress to our bodily system. It is usually due to things related to worldly matters. Attaining peace of mind is the ultimate remedy for such maladies. Loving Allāh ﷻ , having hope in His decree and destiny and fearing His disobedience are the main factors that help us to attain detachment from these worldly affairs that stress us and cause anxiety. Channelling our worldly goals to that of a higher objective in pleasing Allāh 卿, will lead to happiness in this world and the hereafter.

"Those who believed and their hearts find rest in the remembrance of Allāh; behold hearts find rest in the remembrance of Allāh." [13:28]

Satanic whispers persistently work to disrupt us attaining this goal. They constantly fool us and decieve us in believing that matters of this world are most important and happiness lies in those things that contravene Islamic values. We have great wealth, yet we are decieved by satanic whispers that we have nothing and may suffer poverty [2:268]. We therefore, need Allāh's 卿 protection against the evils of His creation that misguide us, causing us to suffer the repercussions of our actions and the actions of others against us.

Sayyidunā Khālid Ibn Walīd ؓ complained to the Holy Prophet ﷺ that he could not sleep because of *al-arq* (insomnia). The Holy Prophet ﷺ told him to recite the following when retiring to bed:

اَللّٰهُمَّ رَبَّ السَّمَوَاتِ السَّبْعِ وَمَا أَظَلَّتْ وَرَبَّ الْأَرَضِينَ وَمَا أَقَلَّتْ وَرَبَّ الشَّيَاطِينِ وَمَا أَضَلَّتْ كُنْ لِي جَارًا مِنْ شَرِّ خَلْقِكَ كُلِّهِمْ جَمِيعًا أَنْ يَفْرُطَ عَلَيَّ أَحَدٌ مِنْهُمْ أَوْ أَنْ يَبْغِيَ عَزَّ جَارُكَ وَجَلَّ ثَنَاؤُكَ وَلَا إِلٰهَ غَيْرُكَ لَا إِلٰهَ إِلَّا أَنْتَ

Trans: "O Allāh, Lord of the seven heavens and what they shade, and Lord of the earths and what they contain, Lord of the devils and what they misguide, be a protection for me from the evil of all Your creation, that any of them wrong me or transgress against me. Honoured is he who is under Your protection; may You be glorified and praised, there is no god beside You, there is no god but You." [Tirmizi]

Practical Advice to Assist One to Sleep
One must remove or treat all the physical things that effect sleep, such as pain, cough, extremes of temperatures and excessive light etc. One must abstain from sins and the influence of bad company, turning to Allāh ﷻ for guidance and relief of worldly anxieties. One must then get into a regular habit of avoiding those things that hinder sleep and take up those measures that promote sleep:

1. Set a routine of times of sleeping and waking up.
2. Only go to bed when tired.
3. Arrange a bed time routine that will associate with sleep, like Dhikr before sleeping and read the above Du'ā (supplication).
4. Do not nap at other inappropriate times.
5. Do not watch television, make phone calls, eat, or work while you are in bed.
6. Rather than worrying about things while you are trying to get to sleep, ponder over Allāh's ﷻ might and power and marvel at His amazing creation.
7. Avoid or limit tea, coffee, chocolate, and smoking as these are stimulants.
8. Do not eat a big meal or spicy foods just before bedtime.
9. A small snack like banana, fish or a warm drink of milk

before bedtime may help.

10. Keeping fit with daily exercise at least 4 hours before you are planning to go to bed will allow you to cool down.

11. Do not lie in bed becoming anxious about sleeping. Instead, get up and go to another room for a short period and do something else, such as reading the Holy Qur'ān or listen to some recitation or Islamic recordings.

Finally, confide in Allāh ﷻ and have trust that He will heal and bring back this great blessing of sleep into your life.

Allāh ﷻ Knows Best

Cupping - Hijāmah
Dr Rafaqat Rashid

Q What is Hijāmah?

A The word Hijāmah (cupping) comes from the word Hajm which means sucking. Technically, it refers to the extraction of blood, particularly at the nape of the neck, by means of a vessel, after making an incision in the appropriate part of the skin. Cupping has been practiced since ancient times by the Egyptians, Chinese and Greeks. It was a form of treatment which grew from humoral medicine related to the balance of the four "humors" in the body: blood, phlegm, yellow bile and black bile. This used to be an influential form of medical treatment in Europe and the Middle-Eastern countries in past centuries. There was also a surge of cupping in European medicine during the 18-19th centuries. So what are the benefits of cupping?

Spiritual Benefits of Cupping

Cupping is a Sunnah of our beloved Prophet ﷺ. Sayyidunā Jābir Ibn Abdullāh ؓ narrates that he heard the Holy Prophet ﷺ say, "If there is anything good in the medicines that you treat yourselves with, then this good is in the incision of the cupper, or a drink of honey or cauterization with fire, but I do not like to be cauterized."

[Bukhāri, Muslim]

On the night of Isrā (the night ascension to the heavens), the Holy Prophet ﷺ did not pass any angel except that the angel said to him, "O' Muhammad, order your Ummah with Hijāmah." [Tirmizi]

Contemporary Fiqh   Cupping - Hijāmah

Physical Benefits of Cupping

Cupping can also cure and heal physical ailments. The Holy Prophet ﷺ said, "Healing is in three things: drinking honey, incision of a cupper, and cauterizing with fire, but I do not permit my Ummah to use cautery."   [Bukhāri]

Sayyidunā Anas Ibn Mālik ؓ narrates that the Holy Prophet ﷺ was treated with cupping by Abū Taybah and he would say, "The best medicine to treat oneself with is cupping or, it is one of the best."   [Bukhāri]

Sayyidunā Abū Hurairah ؓ narrates that the Holy Prophet ﷺ said, "If there is anything good to be used as a remedy, then it is cupping (Hijāmah)."   [Abū Dāwūd, Ibn Mājah]

Cupping has been claimed to have many benefits, some of the main ones are as follows, as mentioned in Zād Al-Ma'ād of Ibnul-Qayyim ﵀:

1. Circulatory diseases and high blood pressure

2. Headaches
Sayyidunā Salmā ؓ narrates that whenever someone complained of a headache to the Holy Prophet ﷺ, he would advise them to perform cupping (Hijāmah).   [Abū Dāwūd]

3. Pain in the neck, stomach and rheumatic pain in the muscles
Sayyidunā Abdullāh Ibn Abbās ؓ reports that a Jewish woman gave poisoned meat to the Holy Prophet ﷺ. When the Holy Prophet ﷺ felt pain from it, he performed cupping. He once travelled

173

whilst in the state of Ihrām and felt the same pain, so he performed cupping. [Ahmad]

4. Pains in joints

Sayyidunā Jābir ؓ reported that the Holy Prophet ﷺ fell from his horse onto the trunk of a palm tree and dislocated his foot. The Holy Prophet ﷺ was cupped on (his foot) because of the bruising. [Ibn Mājah]

5. Black magic

Ibnul Qayyim ؒ states that the Holy Prophet ﷺ was cupped on his head when he was afflicted with black magic and this is the best cure for this, if performed correctly. [Zādul-Ma'ād]

The Procedure

Hijāmah is of three types:

- **Dry cupping** - A vacuum vessel (usually made of glass) is used on different areas of the body to gather the blood around that area and no incision is made, just small, light scratches using a razor.

- **Dry massage cupping** - This is no different to dry cupping except olive oil is applied to the skin before applying the cups.

- **Wet cupping** - This again is like dry cupping except, incisions are made in order to remove harmful blood.

Best Times for Cupping

Sayyidunā Abdullāh Ibn Umar ⁕ narrates that the Holy Prophet ﷺ said, "Cupping on an empty stomach (after fasting) is best. There is a cure and a blessing in it and it improves the intellect and the memory, so perform cupping, with Allāh's ﷻ blessings, on Thursdays. For reasons of safety, do not perform cupping on Wednesday, Friday, Saturday and Sunday. Also perform cupping on Monday and Tuesday, for these are the days that Allāh ﷻ saved Prophet Ayyūb ﷺ from a trial and inflicted him with the trial on Wednesday." [Ibn Mājah]

Sayyidunā Anas Ibn Mālik ⁕ narrates that the Holy Prophet ﷺ also said, "Whoever performs cupping on the 17th, 19th or 21st day (of the Islamic month), then it is a cure for every disease." [Abū Dāwūd, Ibn Mājah]

Areas of the Body for Cupping

The Holy Prophet ﷺ was treated with cupping three times at the side and base of his neck. [Abū Dāwūd, Ibn Mājah]

The Holy Prophet ﷺ was cupped on his head. [Bukhāri]

The Holy Prophet ﷺ was cupped on his hips because of hip pain and on the top of his foot because of foot pain. [Abū Dāwūd]

Ibnul Qayyim ﷺ mentions in Zādul-Ma'ād, a number of sites where cupping can be performed to benefit different ailments.

Conclusion

Unfortunately, the practice of cupping (Hijāmah) has slowly declined with time, even in Arab countries. The practice of Hijāmah exists today, but in a non-professional capacity, resulting in reluctance to accept its regular practice. China has held on to the practice of cupping in a professional capacity which has shown good results.

Although large, expensive, high quality trials have not been conducted in relation to the effectiveness of cupping, clinical studies have shown that the use of cupping in a complementary medical setting benefits patients with pain, shingles, asthma, cough, general flu symptoms and many more ailments.

One thing is clear for us as Muslims, Hijāmah as was practiced at the time of our beloved Prophet ﷺ, is spiritually and physically beneficial and to perform such a procedure is to revive a Sunnah of our beloved Prophet ﷺ, which is rewarding in itself.

I finish with a word of caution, that if one does wish to be treated with Hijāmah, then he should seek a well-trained cupper with experience. Ideally it should be done with one who is a practicing Muslim as he/she is more likely to carry out the procedure with minimal risk and in the method prescribed by our beloved Prophet ﷺ.

Allāh ﷻ Knows Best

Sending Dead Relatives Abroad for Burial
Dr Rafaqat Rashid

Q I have been told by some people that sending the body of dead relatives back home, abroad, requires the body to have alcohol pumped into it. Is this true? What is your opinion about how Muslims should deal with this when under pressure by relatives?

A This is a very sensitive area, especially for those who have had a close relative pass away, having left a final wish, that they would want to be buried abroad in their country of origin. Unfortunately, it is a common problem. Due to the associated sensitivities, I shall be very factual, unbiased and relay the least amount of opinion, leaving you to decide what you think should be done. Firstly, I will briefly explain the legal procedure after death and what Muslims should do to make the process smoother. I shall outline the procedures in repatriating (transporting) dead bodies abroad. Then, I shall outline the Islamic principles related to such procedures and finally, I shall conclude by giving you some pointers on how to deal with relatives on such issues.

1. Legal Procedures After Death
The process of certifying death is the most important step in ensuring everything is set in motion and on time. Muslim relatives of the deceased should try to ensure prompt and suitable arrangements are made to get hold of a death certificate signed by a doctor. This can be troublesome on a weekend because of the availability of doctors and the coroner during this time, or if the deceased has not

Contemporary Fiqh   Transporting the Deceased Abroad

been seen alive by a doctor 14 days prior to death. It is very likely, that if this criteria is not fulfilled, a post-mortem will be required. This is a legal requirement and relatives have very little say in the matter. Once the "Cause of Death Certificate" is issued, the death must be registered with the Registrar for deaths. An appointment is usually required but Registrars can be helpful and flexible in sensitive situations.

If the intention is to repatriate the deceased abroad, then the Coroner must be informed and will issue a certificate (form 104), so that the body can be repatriated abroad. The Coroner will require the undertaker's details, a schedule of movement, flight details to the final destination and a copy of the death certificate to do this. This process can cause delays depending on the availability of the coroner and the level of complications related to the case.

The next stage is for the undertakers to arrange embalming or treatment of the deceased before travelling abroad. This is a legal requirement and the shipping airline will require a certificate before they accept the body. This process is carried out by a professional embalmer and can take up to 2 hours. It is done before the Ghusl (bath) and Janāzah (funeral prayer). A full payment is also required by the undertakers prior to the repatriation. Full embalming is legally obligatory as is the use of a zinc lined coffin or metal casket. I shall now explain the embalming procedure:

2. The Embalming Procedure
The body is placed on the mortuary table, on its back with the

Contemporary Fiqh

Transporting the Deceased Abroad

head elevated with a head block. All clothing is removed and sometimes, a modesty cloth may be placed on the genitals. The body is then washed with a germicide-insecticide. This is placed inside the nose and mouth cavities also, which are then filled with gauze or cotton to absorb fluid and debris. The body is then stretched, flexed and massaged to prevent body stiffness (rigor mortis). The eyes are closed using an eye cap to set them and the mouth is held closed by either using sutures, wires or an adhesive.

The actual embalming process consists of 4 stages:

1. <u>Arterial Embalming</u> - This is when formaldehyde, methanol, ethanol (that is between 10-60% alcohol) and other solvents are pumped into the arteries of the neck and drained from the veins in the neck to form a circulation of fluid to release clots, preserve, sanitise and disinfect the whole bodily circulation.

2. <u>Cavity Embalming</u> - This is when a trocar (a long metal hose device) is pushed through the skin just above the navel and driven into the chest and the abdominal cavities, puncturing the organs and releasing their fluids and debris. The cavities are then filled with concentrated chemicals containing formaldehyde.

3. <u>Hypodermic Embalming</u> - Embalming solution is then injected under the skin in all appropriate areas.

4. <u>Surface Embalming</u> - This is when the solution is supplemented with other methods to mask scars, injured body parts or infested areas.

3. Islamic Issues Related to Such Procedures
The following Islamic notions are potentially violated in such a process:

1. Delay of funeral and burial. It is an essential aspect of the rights of the deceased that they are bathed and shrouded and a funeral prayer is offered according to the Sunnah and as soon as is possible. This is to express respect to the deceased and to give them a dignified burial.

To attain such dignity, the Ulamā have made it clear that the burial should take place at the same burial ground as the place of death, or the most convenient place in its vicinity. To transport the body elsewhere, without a valid excuse, is considered prohibited (Makrūh Tahrīmi). [Raddul-Muhtār, Hāshia Tahtāwī alā Marāqī al-Falāh, Bahr ur-Rā'iq]

2. According to the Hanafi school, to perform more than one Janāzah is not permitted, except in exceptional cases, with the permission of the Wali, though the same person cannot read the same Janāzah on the same body more than once. [Raddul-Muhtār, I'lā us-Sunan]

3. The body should not be defiled as this is Hurma of the body (violating the dignity of the body), which is prohibited in Islām. This includes cutting, piercing the body, placing impure substances into the body or taking organs from the body. Breaking the bones of the dead is like breaking the bones of the living.

[Muslim, Abū Dāwūd, Ibn Mājah]

4. To leave the body uncovered, exposing genitalia is undignified and violates human dignity and integrity.

5. Transporting and carrying the body in cargo and from place to place without a valid excuse is to dishonour and violate the right owed to the deceased and Allāh ﷻ, as it is delaying burial and causing inconvenience.

6. Spending large sums of money to perform procedures on the body that are considered prohibited, is also a waste and a violation of Islamic principles.

4. Conclusion
It is clear that the process of repatriating the deceased from country to country does not benefit the relatives or the deceased when seen from an Islamic perspective. Such acts are performed out of emotion and have no basis in Islām. My suggestion is that the embalming procedure should be explained to relatives sensitively and a greater awareness be made of such practices, so that even for those who have made a last wish, their relatives will be reluctant to undergo such a process after death.

Allāh ﷻ Knows Best

Isāl-e-Thawāb - (Sending the Reward to the Deceased)

By Mufti Abdul Waheed

Q I want to know about Isāl-e-Thawāb as I read somewhere that it is Bid'ah. What does Islām say about Isāl-e-Thawāb? If it is permissible, then what are the ways to do Isāl-e-Thawāb?

A The most preferred opinion, according to the Ahlus-Sunnah wal-Jamā'at, is that Isāl-e-Thawāb is permissible. However, there are many forms and methods of performing this act. Unfortunately, due to the prevalence of ignorance, many people, either deny it totally, or become extreme as well as over exaggerate in this matter. There are some aspects of Ibādah that, although are permissible, are performed in a manner that conflicts with the Holy Qur'ān and Sunnah, due to which, it renders the entire practice as void and deprived from attaining the rewards. Amongst those practices is Isāl-e-Thawāb. This is because such perpetrators do not follow the Islamic guidelines properly and employ their own methods and modes that conform to their own desires.

Since this topic requires an elaborated discussion, I will therefore, outline in this treatise, the different forms of performing virtuous acts with the intention of Isāl-e-Thawāb, its correct application, evidences from the Holy Qur'ān and Sunnah and its guidelines and parameters. Hopefully, by the end of this treatise, the inquisitive reader will have a good understating of this concept and its limits.

Contemporary Fiqh — Isāl-e-Thawāb

What is Isāl-e-Thawāb?

To perform a virtuous act which has been established from the Holy Qur'ān and Sunnah and thereafter, to transmit the reward attained from that ritual act to another person, whether he is alive or deceased is Isāl-e-Thawāb.

The conditions for its permissibility are:

1) Imān - The one who sends the reward must have Imān. If he has no Imān, then how can the deceased receive the reward if he himself is deprived from reward? Likewise, the person to whom the reward will be sent must be a Muslim. A non-Muslim cannot receive the reward of any action when it is apparently known that he died without Imān.

2) The one who sends the reward of a particular virtuous act should himself act upon it. For some people, such practices are only at the time of sending the reward and they do not practice it primarily for themselves on any other occasions.

3) To ensure that the practice and its method must be in accordance (and not conflicting) with the teachings of the Holy Qur'ān and Sunnah. If the action itself is an innovation in Dīn, then how can the deceased receive the reward if those practicing it will not attain the reward themselves?

Nevertheless, the scholars state that after sending the reward, the sender's reward will not diminish; he will also receive the full reward of his action.

Sayyidunā Abdullāh Ibn Umar ﷠ relates that the Holy Prophet ﷺ said, "If each one of you gives optional charity, then he should give it on behalf of his parents so that both receive the reward, whilst his reward will not diminish in anything." (Sharhus Sudūr)

Another report explains that if a person initiates a good practice whilst others follow him, then he will also receive a share of their reward without their reward diminishing. The Holy Prophet ﷺ said, "Whosoever initiates an excellent Sunnah practice, then for him is the reward (of that act) and the reward of the one who acts upon it, without his (the one who acts upon it) reward diminishing in anything." (Muslim)

As mentioned previously, there are many ways of benefitting other Muslims, whether alive or deceased, in worship. Some are as follows:

1. Benefitting the Living or Deceased Muslim Through Du'ā
The scholars of the Ahlus-Sunnah wal-Jamā'at are unanimous that to make Du'ā for another Muslim, whether dead or alive, is permissible. There are ample amounts of Qur'anic verses and Ahādīth that give evidence to its permissibility:

Allāh ﷻ states, **"O our Lord forgive us and our brothers who have preceded us in faith."** (59:10)

Allāh ﷻ also states, **"And say, 'O my Lord, show mercy to them both (parents) just as they nurtured me in my childhood.'"** (17:24)

Allāh ﷻ quotes the Du'ā of Sayyidunā Ibrāhīm ﷺ as follows, **"O our Lord forgive me and my parents and the believers on the Day when the reckoning shall take place."(14:41)**

These verses of the Holy Qur'ān are enough to prove the point of supplicating for someone else to be permissible. Therefore, I will suffice with the above.

2. Benefitting the Living or Deceased Muslim Through a Virtuous Act

To carry out a meritorious act and then to pass on the reward to the living or deceased Muslim can be sub-divided into two categories:

a) Those actions where there is a direct connection between the living or the deceased and the action.

A virtuous deed that the deceased did whilst he was alive and becomes a remnant act on his behalf, to the extent that after his death, others are still benefitting from his virtuous act and works. The scholars of the Ahlus-Sunnah wal-Jamā'at unanimously agree that as long as others are benefitting from his virtuous deed, the deceased is continuously receiving the share of reward. The evidence of this category are as follows:

■ Sayyidunā Abū Hurairah ﷺ relates that the Holy Prophet ﷺ said, "When a person passes away, then all his actions come to an end except for three: (1) Ongoing continuous charity, (2) Knowledge from which benefit is sought, (3) A pious son who supplicates for him." (Muslim)

■ Sayyidunā Abū Hurairah ﷺ relates that the Holy Prophet ﷺ said,

"Verily, a believer who receives the reward of his good deeds after his death are; knowledge that he taught and propagated, a pious child he left behind, the Holy Qur'ān he left as inheritance, a Masjid he constructed, a house he had built for the traveller, a river (or well) he made, or a charity that he gave whilst he was alive and in good health, then the reward (of all the above deeds) will reach him after his death." (Ibn Mājah)

- Sayyidunā Jarīr Ibn Abdullāh ⁂ relates that the Holy Prophet ⁂ said, "Whosoever initiates an excellent Sunnah practice in Islām, then for him is the reward and the reward of those who act upon it after him, without their reward diminishing and whosoever initiates an evil practice, then he will bear the burden of sin and the sins of those who practice it, without the sin diminishing in anything." (Muslim)

b) Those deeds where there is no direct connection between the deceased and the action but another person sends the reward to the deceased.

There are many examples of such nature in the authentic Ahādīth. Sayyidunā Abdullāh Ibn Abbās ⁂ narrates that once the Holy Prophet ⁂ passed by two graves in which the inhabitants were being punished. The Holy Prophet ⁂ took a branch that was fresh. He broke it into two pieces and placed each one on the head-side of both graves. The Sahābah ⁂ enquired as to why he did that. The Holy Prophet ⁂ replied, "With the hope that they will alleviate their punishment as long as they do not become dry."

(Bukhāri, Muslim)

Contemporary Fiqh   Isāl-e-Thawāb

In this Hadīth, the Holy Prophet ﷺ engraved a small twig onto the head side, with the hope that it will benefit the deceased, so long as it remains fresh. A fresh twig makes Tasbīh of Allāh ﷻ though humans may not comprehend it. This proves that a good deed can affect the inhabitants of the graves where there is no direct connection between the inhabitants and the action of a person.

This category subdivides into various methods of sending reward to the deceased person. They can be sent to a living person also;

1. Monetary Worship
To send the reward of any form of monetary worship such as optional charity, Qurbāni etc to another Muslim is permissible.

Sayyidunā Abū Hurairah ﷺ narrates that a man said to the Holy Prophet ﷺ, "Verily my father has passed away and has not bequeathed anything regarding the wealth he has left behind, so will it suffice for him if I give some of it as Sadaqah?" The Holy Prophet ﷺ said, "Yes." (Muslim)

Sayyidah Ā'ishah ﷺ narrates that a man approached the Holy Prophet ﷺ and said, "O Messenger of Allāh ﷺ! My mother has suddenly passed away and has not bequeathed her wealth and I assume that if I had spoken to her (before she passed away), then she would have given it to charity, so if I spend it on charity on her behalf, would she receive the reward?" He replied, "Yes."
(Bukhāri, Muslim)

Sayyidunā Abdullāh Ibn Abbās ؓ relates that the mother of Sa'd Ibn Ubādah ؓ passed away during his absence. He went to the Holy Prophet ﷺ and said, "O Messenger of Allāh ﷺ! My mother passed away during my absence, so if I give Sadaqah on her behalf will it benefit her in any way?" He replied, "Yes." Sa'd ؓ said, "Then I make you a witness that I have given my orchard as Sadaqah on behalf of her." (Bukhāri)

Sayyidunā Abdullāh Ibn Amr Ibn Ās ؓ relates that my grandfather Ās Ibn Wā'il bequeathed to emancipate one hundred slaves, so his son, Hishām Ibn Ās (who was a non-Musim), emancipated fifty and his other son, Amr Ibn Ās ؓ intended to emancipate the remaining fifty. He said, "Not until I have asked the Holy Prophet ﷺ." So he approached the Holy Prophet ﷺ and said, "O Messenger of Allāh ﷺ! My father bequeathed to emancipate one hundred slaves and Hishām has emancipated fifty and fifty remains, so can I emancipate them on his behalf?" The Holy Prophet ﷺ said, "If he (Ās Ibn Wā'il) was a Muslim and you emancipated a slave, gave charity for him or did Hajj on his behalf, then the reward would have surely reached him." (Abū Dāwūd)

To Perform Qurbāni with the Intention of Isāl-e-Thawāb.

Sayyidah Ā'ishah ؓ narrates that the Holy Prophet ﷺ, on one occasion, performed Qurbāni of a bulky healthy ram with horns and he said, whilst slaughtering, "In the Name of Allāh, O Allāh accept this from Muhammad, from the family of Muhammad and from the Ummah of Muhammad." (Muslim)

Contemporary Fiqh   Isāl-e-Thawāb

Sayyidunā Abū Hurairah ؓ narrates that when the Holy Prophet ﷺ would intend to perform Qurbāni, then he would purchase two huge, bulky, healthy, castrated rams with horns that were black, with some whiteness effect. He would sacrifice one of them from Muhammad and the family of Muhammad and the other on behalf of his Ummah who affirm Tawhīd and affirm in his message." (Fathul Bāri)

Based on the above evidences, the scholars of Ahlus-Sunnah wal-Jamā'at unanimously agree upon the permissibility of Isāl-e-Thawāb through monetary worship.

Shaykhul Islām Ibn Taymiyah ﷺ states, "The Imāms are unanimous that (the reward of) Sadaqah reaches the deceased and similarly, monetary worship, such as freeing a slave."

(Fatāwa Ibn Taymiyah)

Mufti Shafī Sāhib ﷺ states that the most superior and preferred method of Isāl-e-Thawāb is through monetary worship because the scholars of Ahlus-Sunnah wal-Jamā'at have unanimously agreed upon its permissibility, whereas, in the case of physical worship there are some differences of opinion amongst the jurists.

(Jawāhirul Fiqh)

2. Physical Worship

Physical form of worship include fasting, Salāh, reciting the Holy Qur'ān, Tasbīh etc. In relation to this method, there is a difference of opinion amongst the four schools of thought;

Imām Shāfi'ī ﷺ and Imām Mālik ﷺ view that Isāl-e-Thawāb through physical worship, such as Holy Qur'ān recitation, is not permissible because of the statement of Allāh ﷻ, **"For a man is not but what he strove for."** (53:39)

Imām Abū Hanīfah ﷺ and Imām Ahmad ﷺ are of the opinion that Isāl-e-Thawāb through physical worship is permissible. The verse of the Holy Qur'ān presented by Imām Shāfi'ī ﷺ refers to Imān and not physical worship, otherwise, other forms of Isāl-e-Thawāb, such as monetary worship, should also come under this category. In support of the Hanafi position on this matter, the evidences are as follows:

A woman whose mother before passing away, vowed to offer Salāh in Masjid Qubā but could not fulfill her oath, was instructed by Sayyidunā Abdullāh Ibn Umar ﷺ to offer Salāh in Masjid Qubā on her behalf. (Bukhāri)

Sayyidunā Abū Hurairah ﷺ once remarked, "Is there anyone amongst you who will take the responsibility on my behalf to offer two or four Rak'ats in Masjid Ishār and say that this is for Abū Hurairah?" (Abū Dāwūd)

One Sahābi ﷺ asked the Holy Prophet ﷺ about how he can maintain respect for his parents after their demise. The Holy Prophet ﷺ replied, "That you offer Salāh with your optional Salāh and you fast for them with your optional fast." (Dār Qutni)

Sayyidunā Abū Hurairah ⬥ relates from the Holy Prophet ⬥ that whosoever recites Sūrah Al-Fātihah, Sūrah Al-Ikhlās, Sūrah At-Takāthur and thereafter says, "O Allāh, verily, I have sent the reward of my recitation of Your Words to the graves of the male and female believers," they shall intercede on his behalf.

(Sharhus-Sudūr)

The Holy Prophet ⬥ said, "Recite Sūrah Yāseen upon the deceased." (Majma-uz-Zawā'id)

Sayyidunā Anas Ibn Mālik ⬥ narrates that the Holy Prophet ⬥ said, "When Sūrah Yāsīn is recited upon the people of the grave, Allāh ⬥ alleviates their punishment." (Tafsīr Mazhari)

The Holy Prophet ⬥ said, "Whosoever passes by the cemetery (of the Muslims) and recites Sūrah Al-Ikhlās eleven times and sends the reward to the deceased, then he shall receive the reward equal to the number of the graves." (Kashful Khifā)

3. Combination of Monetary and Physical Worship

To send the reward of such a virtuous act that is a combination of physical and monetary worship (e.g. Hajj) has also been established from many Ahādīth.

Sayyidunā Abdullāh Ibn Abbās ⬥ relates that a woman once approached the Holy Prophet ⬥ and said, "Verily, my mother vowed to perform Hajj but did not perform it until she passed away, so can I perform Hajj on her behalf?" The Holy Prophet ⬥ replied, "Perform Hajj on her behalf." (Bukhāri)

The scholars are unanimous that Hajj is the only form of worship in which (as well as optional Hajj), to perform a Fardh Hajj on behalf of the deceased is permissible. If Hajj was Fardh upon them but they were unable to discharge their obligation throughout their lifetime due to unforeseen circumstances and before they passed away, they made a will for someone to perform Hajj on their behalf, this is known as Hajj-Badl (substitute Hajj).

The scholars have elaborated on this topic and outlined its conditions but at the moment, this is not our topic of discussion. The main point of concern here is that, if a Fardh Hajj can be performed on behalf of a living or deceased person, whilst meeting all the necessary conditions, then an optional Hajj on behalf of someone else is also permissible. (See Raddul Muhtār for more details on this subject).

Some Important Injunctions about Isāl-e-Thawāb
By now, it has become clear that there are different forms of Isāl-e-Thawāb established in the light of many authentic Ahādīth. Nevertheless, one must keep in mind that Isāl-e-Thawāb is Mustahab and a highly recommended practice. To consider it obligatory and necessary, is itself a form of exaggeration in Dīn. Nowadays, many people have become extreme in this practice and have introduced many baseless traditions and methods. It has come to a point where its permissibility has become questionable amongst many people.

One must not become so hasty in condemning an act or denying the entire concept, based on the practice of the general public. Rather, it is necessary to primarily seek guidance and gain insight of such

Contemporary Fiqh — Isāl-e-Thawāb

matters in light of the Holy Qur'ān and Sunnah and the statements of the Fuqahā (Islamic Jurists). Isāl-e-Thawāb is among those issues which some minorities totally reject, based on the practice of the general public. It is a known fact that many people, due to ignorance, have become extreme in certain virtuous practices. However, rather than totally rejecting the concept, such people must be pointed towards the right direction of its correct method. In this way, they will not be deprived from attaining its benefits and rewards.

Just as every form of worship consists of rules and guidelines, similarly, the practice of Isāl-e-Thawāb contains some guiding principles. Those principles are as follows:

1) Isāl-e-Thawāb is not permitted in Innovated Practices
Isāl-e-Thawāb is permissible in those actions that are established in Shari'ah (e.g. Dhikr, optional Salāh and fasting, Hajj, Sadaqah etc.) Innovated practices cannot be practiced with the intention of Isāl-e -Thawāb, such as Ghiyārvi, Chāleeswa etc. If the person practicing an innovated act is deprived from the reward, then how can he send that reward to the deceased? Therefore, the act must be established from the sources of Shari'ah.

2) Not to restrict Dhikr and Recitation of the Holy Qur'ān with the Intention of Isāl-e-Thawāb in the form of congregation.
For people to congregate for Dhikr and recitation, with the intention of Isāl-e-Thawāb, it would be permissible only if people congregate without considering it to be necessary, not compelling anyone to attend the congregation, not to criticize those that do not

Contemporary Fiqh   Isāl-e-Thawāb

wish to attend, not considering it a Sunnah act, not restricting it to a date and time, not to recite audibly, whereby it disturbs others and the Holy Qur'ān is respected. (Fatāwa Rahīmiyyah)

If any of the above conditions are violated, then it would not be permissible. This can be derived from the statement of the Fuqahā, in relation to congregational Dhikr:

"The scholars of the past and present (Salaf and Khalaf) are unanimous upon the Istihbāb (preferred act) of Dhikr in congregation in the Masjid or elsewhere, without objecting (against others) as long as the audible Dhikr will not interrupt a person who is sleeping or engaged in Salāh or recitation." (Raddul Muhtār)

What is clear from the above text is that congregational Dhikr (or recitation) itself is permissible. Likewise, collective Dhikr with the intention of Isāl-e-Thawāb, would be permissible as long as the congregational method is not considered necessary. Even individual recitation and Dhikr is also sufficient.

The above was to merely explain the general principle but due to the prevalent practice of this method, people have now considered it as something necessary and introduced other innovated acts such as Ghiyārvi and Chāleeswa etc. Not only do they strictly adhere to it but they also pressurize others to participate.

Those that do not wish to participate are ridiculed, despised and condemned as Wahābis. I believe that this type of approach is incorrect because for something that Shari'ah has not emphasized, no one has the right to emphasize it.

Congregational Dhikr can be considered as a Mustahab act but nothing higher. To consider it necessary, is a form of exaggeration in Dīn which then becomes an innovation. If something becomes an innovated act, then neither do the participants receive the reward, nor does it reach the deceased.

In regards to sending the reward of Dhikr and recitation of the Holy Qur'ān, Shaykh Ashraf Ali Thānwi ﷺ makes an excellent suggestion as follows:

The current method of the Holy Qur'ān recitation with the intention of Isāl-e-Thawāb is not correct. Rather, close family relatives and friends should be requested to send Isāl-e-Thawāb individually, whatever is in their ability, even if it means reciting Sūrah Al-Ikhlās thrice for Isāl-e-Thawāb.

A congregational method like this is highly inappropriate. It would be better to recite Sūrah Al-Ikhlās individually than completing ten Qur'āns in congregation, because its level of sincerity is not high as compared to individually reciting.

Allāh ﷻ does not observe the quantity of Ibādah, rather, He observes the level of sincerity within the Ibādah. The Holy Prophet ﷺ said, "If someone spends in charity equivalent to the mountain of Uhud, then his reward can never become parallel to my Companion who spends the equivalent of a handful of dates in charity." The difference is due to the level of piety and sincerity.

(Fatāwa Rahīmiyyah)

What would be highly recommended is, rather than congregating everyone for the recitation of the Holy Qur'ān, each person should be requested to recite individually, some portions of the Holy Qur'ān, such as Sūrah Yāsīn, Sūrah Al-Fātihah, Sūrah Al-Ikhlās etc. or a Juz from the Holy Qur'ān in whatever suitable and convenient time available for them. Thereafter, they may send the reward to the deceased person and for the entire Muslim Ummah who have died upon Imān. In this way, the conditions stipulated above are not infringed and the prime objective, which is Isāl-e-Thawāb is also achieved.

3) Seek forgiveness for the deceased in the graveyard

Once the deceased person is buried, then it would be permissible to make Istighfār for him/her upon the grave.

Sayyidunā Uthmān Ibn Affān ﷺ narrates that when the Holy Prophet ﷺ would complete the burial of the deceased, he would stand by the grave and say, "Seek forgiveness for your brother and ask Allāh ﷻ to grant him firmness because he is now being questioned." (Abū Dāwūd)

The supplication can be made individually or collectively by the grave. The Fuqahā state that when supplicating for the deceased by his grave, it is necessary to face the Qiblah. It is stated in Fatāwa Hindiyyah, "When a person intends to do Du'ā, then he should stand facing the Qiblah." The wisdom in this is so that it does not give the impression of praying to the dead.

Contemporary Fiqh　　　　　　　　　　　　Isāl-e-Thawāb

It is also permissible to recite some verses of the Holy Qur'ān or Tasbīhāt whilst in the cemetery. The graveyard is not a restricted location for Isāl-e-Thawāb for the deceased. Even if a person is at home, he can carry out Isāl-e-Thawāb. Similarly, there is no specific time for Isāl-e-Thawāb; a person is at liberty to do it whatever time or day is convenient for him. It is totally forbidden to revere the graves of the pious people, for example, performing Tawāf around their graves, prostrating over their graves, sitting on their graves out of respect, putting food on their graves, facing their graves and directly beseeching for their assistance, erecting tombs over their graves and so on. Such practices are Shirk and a major sin.

Conclusion

In conclusion, there are many forms of Isāl-e-Thawāb and each method has been established from Ahādīth. However, this is also followed by some guided principles and strict conditions. All forms of Isāl-e-Thawāb are permissible as long as the conditions mentioned are not infringed. If any of these conditions are breached, then that would render the entire practice as void and deprived of reward.

Allāh ﷻ Knows Best

Other titles from JKN Publications

Your Questions Answered
An outstanding book written by Shaykh Mufti Saiful Islām. A very comprehensive yet simple Fatāwa book and a source of guidance that reaches out to a wider audience i.e. the English speaking Muslims. The reader will benefit from the various answers to questions based on the Laws of Islām relating to the beliefs of Islām, knowledge, Sunnah, pillars of Islām, marriage, divorce and contemporary issues.

UK RRP: £7.50

Hadīth for Beginners
A concise Hadīth book with various Ahādeeth that relate to basic Ibādāh and moral etiquettes in Islām accessible to a wider readership. Each Hadīth has been presented with the Arabic text, its translation and commentary to enlighten the reader, its meaning and application in day-to-day life.

UK RRP: £3.00

Du'a for Beginners
This book contains basic Du'ās which every Muslim should recite on a daily basis. Highly recommended to young children and adults studying at Islamic schools and Madrasahs so that one may cherish the beautiful treasure of supplications of our beloved Prophet ﷺ in one's daily life, which will ultimately bring peace and happiness in both worlds, Inshā-Allāh.

UK RRP: £2.00

How well do you know Islām?
An exciting educational book which contains 300 multiple questions and answers to help you increase your knowledge on Islām! Ideal for the whole family, especially children and adult students to learn new knowledge in an enjoyable way and cherish the treasures of knowledge that you will acquire from this book. A very beneficial tool for educational syllabus.

UK RRP: £3.00

Treasures of the Holy Qur'an
This book entitled "Treasures of the Holy Qur'ān" has been compiled to create a stronger bond between the Holy Qur'ān and the readers. It mentions the different virtues of Sūrahs and verses from the Holy Qur'ān with the hope that the readers will increase their zeal and enthusiasm to recite and inculcate the teachings of the Holy Qur'ān into their daily lives.

UK RRP: £3.00

Other titles from JKN PUBLICATIONS

Marriage - A Complete Solution

Islām regards marriage as a great act of worship. This book has been designed to provide the fundamental teachings and guidelines of all what relates to the marital life in a simplified English language. It encapsulates in a nutshell all the marriage laws mentioned in many of the main reference books in order to facilitate their understanding and implementation.

UK RRP: £5.00

Contemporary Fiqh

This book is a comprehensive commentary of Sūrah Luqmān, written beautifully by Shaykh Mufti Saiful Islām. It offers the reader with an enquiring mind, Abūndance of advice, guidance, counselling and wisdom.

The reader will be enlightened by many wonderful topics and anecdotes mentioned in this book, which will create a greater understanding of the Holy Qur'ān and its wisdom. The book highlights some of the wise sayings and words of advice Luqmān ؑ gave to his son.

UK RRP: £3.00

Arabic Grammar for Beginners

This book is a study of Arabic Grammar based on the subject of Nahw (Syntax) in a simplified English format. If a student studies this book thoroughly, he/she will develop a very good foundation in this field, Inshā-Allāh. Many books have been written on this subject in various languages such as Arabic, Persian and Urdu. However, in this day and age there is a growing demand for this subject to be available in English .

UK RRP: £3.00

A Gift to My Youngsters

This treasure filled book, is a collection of Islāmic stories, morals and anecdotes from the life of our beloved Prophet ﷺ, his Companions ؓ and the pious predecessors. The stories and anecdotes are based on moral and ethical values, which the reader will enjoy sharing with their peers, friends, families and loved ones.

"A Gift to My Youngsters" – is a wonderful gift presented to the readers personally, by the author himself, especially with the youngsters in mind. He has carefully selected stories and anecdotes containing beautiful morals, lessons and valuable knowledge and wisdom.

UK RRP: £5.00

Travel Companion
The beauty of this book is that it enables a person on any journey, small or distant or simply at home, to utilise their spare time to read and benefit from an exciting and vast collection of important and interesting Islamic topics and lessons. Written in simple and easy to read text, this book will immensely benefit both the newly interested person in Islām and the inquiring mind of a student expanding upon their existing knowledge. Inspiring reminders from the Holy Qur'ān and the blessed words of our beloved Prophet ﷺ beautifies each topic and will illuminate the heart of the reader.
UK RRP: £5.00

Pearls of Wisdom
Junaid Baghdādī ؓ once said, "Allāh ﷻ strengthens through these Islamic stories the hearts of His friends, as proven from the Qur'anic verse,
"And all that We narrate unto you of the stories of the Messengers, so as to strengthen through it your heart." (11:120)
Mālik Ibn Dinār ؓ stated that such stories are gifts from Paradise. He also emphasised to narrate these stories as much as possible as they are gems and it is possible that an individual might find a truly rare and invaluable gem among them.
UK RRP: £6.00

Inspirations
This book contains a compilation of selected speeches delivered by Shaykh Mufti Saiful Islām on a variety of topics such as the Holy Qur'ān, Nikāh and eating Halāl. Having previously been compiled in separate booklets, it was decided that the transcripts be gathered together in one book for the benefit of the reader. In addition to this, we have included in this book, further speeches which have not yet been printed.
UK RRP: £6.00

Gift to my Sisters
A thought provoking compilation of very interesting articles including real life stories of pious predecessors, imaginative illustrations, medical advices on intoxicants and rehabilitation and much more. All designed to influence and motivate mothers, sisters, wives and daughters towards an ideal Islamic lifestyle. A lifestyle referred to by our Creator, Allāh ﷻ in the Holy Qur'ān as the means to salvation and ultimate success.
UK RRP: £6.00

Gift to my Brothers
A thought provoking compilation of very interesting articles including real life stories of pious predecessors, imaginative illustrations, medical advices on intoxicants and rehabilitation and much more. All designed to influence and motivate fathers, brothers, husbands and sons towards an ideal Islamic lifestyle. A lifestyle referred to by our Creator, Allāh ﷻ in the Holy Qur'ān as the means to salvation and ultimate success.
UK RRP: £5.00

Heroes of Islām
"In the narratives there is certainly a lesson for people of intelligence (understanding)." (12:111)
A fine blend of Islamic personalities who have been recognised for leaving a lasting mark in the hearts and minds of people.
A distinguishing feature of this book is that the author has selected not only some of the most world and historically famous renowned scholars but also these lesser known and a few who have simply left behind a valuable piece of advice to their nearest and dearest. **UK RRP: £5.00**

Ask a Mufti (3 volumes)
Muslims in every generation have confronted different kinds of challenges. Inspite of that, Islām produced such luminary Ulamā who confronted and responded to the challenges of their time to guide the Ummah to the straight path. "Ask A Mufti" is a comprehensive three volume fatwa book, based on the Hanafi School, covering a wide range of topics related to every aspect of human life such as belief, ritual worship, life after death and contemporary legal topics related to purity, commercial transaction, marriage, divorce, food, cosmetic, laws pertaining to women, Islamic medical ethics and much more.

Should I Follow a Madhab?
Taqleed or following one of the four legal schools is not a new phenomenon. Historically, scholars of great calibre and luminaries, each one being a specialist in his own right, were known to have adhered to one of the four legal schools. It is only in the previous century that a minority group emerged advocating a severe ban on following one of the four major schools.
This book endeavours to address the topic of Taqleed and elucidates why it is necessary to do Taqleed in this day and age. It will also, by the Divine Will of Allāh ﷻ dispel some of the confusion surrounding this topic. **UK RRP: £5.00**

Advice for the Students of Knowledge
Allāh ﷻ describes divine knowledge in the Holy Qur'ān as a 'Light'. Amongst the qualities of light are purity and guidance. The Holy Prophet ﷺ has clearly explained this concept in many blessed Ahādeeth and has also taught us many supplications in which we ask for beneficial knowledge.
This book is a golden tool for every sincere student of knowledge wishing to mould his/her character and engrain those correct qualities in order to be worthy of receiving the great gift of Ilm from Allāh ﷻ. **UK RRP: £3.00**

Stories for Children
"Stories for Children" - is a wonderful gift presented to the readers personally, by the author himself, especially with the young children in mind. The stories are based on moral and ethical values, which the reader will enjoy sharing with their peers, friends, families and loved ones. The aim is to present to the children stories and incidents which contain moral lessons, in order to reform and correct their lives, according to the Holy Qur'ān and Sunnah.
UK RRP: £5.00

Pearls from My Shaykh

This book contains a collection of pearls and inspirational accounts of the Holy Prophet ﷺ, his noble Companions, pious predecessors and some personal accounts and sayings of our well-known contemporary scholar and spiritual guide, Shaykh Mufti Saiful Islām Sāhib. Each anecdote and narrative of the pious predecessors have been written in the way that was narrated by Mufti Saiful Islām Sāhib in his discourses, drawing the specific lessons he intended from telling the story. The accounts from the life of the Shaykh has been compiled by a particular student based on their own experience and personal observation. **UK RRP: £5.00**

Paradise & Hell

This book is a collection of detailed explanation of Paradise and Hell including the state and conditions of its inhabitants. All the details have been taken from various reliable sources. The purpose of its compilation is for the reader to contemplate and appreciate the innumerable favours, rewards, comfort and unlimited luxuries of Paradise and at the same time take heed from the punishment of Hell. Shaykh Mufti Saiful Islām Sāhib has presented this book in a unique format by including the Tafseer and virtues of Sūrah Ar-Rahmān. **UK RRP: £5.00**

Prayers for Forgiveness

Prayers for Forgiveness' is a short compilation of Du'ās in Arabic with English translation and transliteration. This book can be studied after 'Du'ā for Beginners' or as a separate book. It includes twenty more Du'ās which have not been mentioned in the previous Du'ā book. It also includes a section of Du'ās from the Holy Qur'ān and a section from the Ahādeeth. The book concludes with a section mentioning the Ninety-Nine Names of Allāh ﷻ with its translation and transliteration. **UK RRP: £3.00**

Scattered Pearls

This book is a collection of scattered pearls taken from books, magazines, emails and WhatsApp messages. These pearls will hopefully increase our knowledge, wisdom and make us realise the purpose of life. In this book, Mufti Sāhib has included messages sent to him from scholars, friends and colleagues which will be beneficial and interesting for our readers Inshā-Allāh. **UK RRP: £4.00**

Poems of Wisdom

This book is a collection of poems from those who contributed to the Al-Mumin Magazine in the poems section. The Hadeeth mentions "Indeed some form of poems are full of wisdom." The themes of each poem vary between wittiness, thought provocation, moral lessons, emotional to name but a few. The readers will benefit from this immensely and make them ponder over the outlook of life in general.

UK RRP: £4.00

Horrors of Judgement Day
This book is a detailed and informative commentary of the first three Sūrahs of the last Juz namely; Sūrah Naba, Sūrah Nāzi'āt and Sūrah Abasa. These Sūrahs vividly depict the horrific events and scenes of the Great Day in order to warn mankind the end of this world. These Sūrahs are an essential reminder for us all to instil the fear and concern of the Day of Judgement and to detach ourselves from the worldly pleasures. Reading this book allows us to attain the true realization of this world and provides essential advices of how to gain eternal salvation in the Hereafter.
RRP: £5:00

Spiritual Heart
It is necessary that Muslims always strive to better themselves at all times and to free themselves from the destructive maladies. This book focusses on three main spiritual maladies; pride, anger and evil gazes. It explains its root causes and offers some spiritual cures. Many examples from the lives of the pious predecessors are used for inspiration and encouragement for controlling the above three maladies. It is hoped that the purification process of the heart becomes easy once the underlying roots of the above maladies are clearly understood. **UK RRP: £5:00**

Hajj & Umrah for Beginners
This book is a step by step guide on Hajj and Umrah for absolute beginners. Many other additional important rulings (Masāil) have been included that will Insha-Allāh prove very useful for our readers. The book also includes some etiquettes of visiting (Ziyārat) of the Holy Prophet's ﷺ blessed Masjid and his Holy Grave.
UK RRP £3:00

Advice for the Spiritual Travellers
This book contains essential guidelines for a spiritual Murīd to gain some familiarity of the science of Tasawwuf. It explains the meaning and aims of Tasawwuf, some understanding around the concept of the soul, and general guidelines for a spiritual Murīd. This is highly recommended book and it is hoped that it gains wider readership among those Murīds who are basically new to the science of Tasawwuf.
UK RRP £3:00

Don't Worry Be Happy
This book is a compilation of sayings and earnest pieces of advice that have been gathered directly from my respected teacher Shaykh Mufti Saiful Islām Sāhib. The book consists of many valuable enlightenments including how to deal with challenges of life, promoting unity, practicing good manners, being optimistic and many other valuable advices. Our respected Shaykh has gathered this Naseehah from meditating, contemplating, analysing and searching for the gems within Qur'anic verses, Ahādeeth and teachings of our Pious Predecessors. **UK RRP £1:00**

Kanzul Bāri
Kanzul Bāri provides a detailed commentary of the Ahādeeth contained in Saheeh al-Bukhāri. The commentary includes Imām Bukhāri's ﷺ biography, the status of his book, spiritual advice, inspirational accounts along with academic discussions related to Fiqh, its application and differences of opinion. Moreover, it answers objections arising in one's mind about certain Ahādeeth. Inquisitive students of Hadeeth will find this commentary a very useful reference book in the final year of their Ālim course for gaining a deeper understanding of the science of Hadeeth. **UK RRP: £15.00**

How to Become a Friend of Allāh ﷻ
The friends of Allāh ﷻ have been described in detail in the Holy Qur'ān and Āhadeeth. This book endeavours its readers to help create a bond with Allāh ﷻ in attaining His friendship as He is the sole Creator of all material and immaterial things. It is only through Allāh's ﷻ friendship, an individual will achieve happiness in this life and the Hereafter, hence eliminate worries, sadness, depression, anxiety and misery of this world. **UK RRP:**

Gems & Jewels
This book contains a selection of articles which have been gathered for the benefit of the readers covering a variety of topics on various aspects of daily life. It offers precious advice and anecdotes that contain moral lessons. The advice captivates its readers and will extend the narrowness of their thoughts to deep reflection, wisdom and appreciation of the purpose of our existence.
UK RRP: £4.00

End of Time
This book is a comprehensive explanation of the three Sūrahs of Juzz Amma; Sūrah Takweer, Sūrah Infitār and Sūrah Mutaffifeen. This book is a continuation from the previous book of the same author, 'Horrors of Judgement Day'. The three Sūrahs vividly sketch out the scene of the Day of Judgement and describe the state of both the inmates of Jannah and Jahannam. Mufti Saiful Islām Sāhib provides an easy but comprehensive commentary of the three Sūrahs facilitating its understanding for the readers whilst capturing the horrific scene of the ending of the world and the conditions of mankind on that horrific Day. **UK RRP: £5.00**

Andalus (modern day Spain), the long lost history, was once a country that produced many great calibre of Muslim scholars comprising of Mufassirūn, Muhaddithūn, Fuqahā, judges, scientists, philosophers, surgeons, to name but a few. The Muslims conquered Andalus in 711 AD and ruled over it for eight-hundred years. This was known as the era of Muslim glory. Many non-Muslim Europeans during that time travelled to Spain to study under Muslim scholars. The remenances of the Muslim rule in Spain are manifested through their universities, magnificent palaces and Masājid carved with Arabic writings, standing even until today. In this book, Shaykh Mufti Saiful Islām shares some of his valuable experiences he witnessed during his journey to Spain. **UK RRP: £3.00**

Ideal Youth
This book contains articles gathered from various social media avenues; magazines, emails, WhatsApp and telegram messages that provide useful tips of advice for those who have the zeal to learn and consider changing their negative habits and behavior and become better Muslims to set a positive trend for the next generation. **UK RRP:£4:00**

Ideal Teacher
This book contains abundance of precious advices for the Ulamā who are in the teaching profession. It serves to present Islamic ethical principles of teaching and to remind every teacher of their moral duties towards their students. This book will Inshā-Allāh prove to be beneficial for newly graduates and scholars wanting to utilize their knowledge through teaching. **UK RRP:£4:00**

Ideal Student
This book is a guide for all students of knowledge in achieving the excellent qualities of becoming an ideal student. It contains precious advices, anecdotes of our pious predecessors and tips in developing good morals as a student. Good morals is vital for seeking knowledge. A must for all students if they want to develop their Islamic Knowledge. **UK RRP:£4:00**

Ideal Parents
This book contains a wealth of knowledge in achieving the qualities of becoming ideal parents. It contains precious advices, anecdotes of our pious predecessors and tips in developing good parenthood skills. Good morals is vital for seeking knowledge. A must for all parents . **UK RRP:£4:00**

Ideal Couple
This book is a compilation of inspiring stories and articles containing useful tips and life skills for every couple. Marriage life is a big responsibility and success in marriage is only possible if the couple know what it means to be an ideal couple. **UK RRP:£4:00**

Ideal Role Model
This book is a compilation of sayings and accounts of our pious predecessors. The purpose of this book is so we can learn from our pious predecessors the purpose of this life and how to attain closer to the Creator. Those people who inspires us attaining closeness to our Creator are our true role models. A must everyone to read. **UK RRP:£4:00**

Bangladesh- A Land of Natural Beauty
This book is a compilation of our respected Shaykh's journeys to Bangladesh including visits to famous Madāris and Masājid around the country. The Shaykh shares some of his thought provoking experiences and his personal visits with great scholars in Bangladesh.
UK RRP: £4.00

Pearls from the Qur'an
This series begins with the small Sūrahs from 30th Juzz initially, unravelling its heavenly gems, precious advices and anecdotes worthy of personal reflection. It will most definitely benefit both those new to as well as advanced students of the science of Tafsīr. The purpose is to make it easily accessible for the general public in understanding the meaning of the Holy Qur'ān. **UK RRP: £10.00**

When the Heavens Split
This book contains the commentary of four Sūrahs from Juzz Amma namely; Sūrah Inshiqāq, Sūrah Burūj, Sūrah Tāriq and Sūrah A'lā. The first two Sūrahs contain a common theme of capturing the scenes and events of the Last Day and how this world will come to an end. However, all four Sūrahs mentioned, have a connection of the journey of humanity, reflection on nature, how nature changes and most importantly, giving severe warnings to mankind about the punishments and exhorting them to prepare for the Hereafter through good deeds and refraining from sins.
UK RRP: £4.00

The Lady who Spoke the Qur'ān
The Holy Prophet ﷺ was sent as a role model who was the physical form of the Holy Qur'ān. Following the ways of the Holy Prophet ﷺ in every second of our lives is pivotal for success. This booklet tells us the way to gain this success. It also includes an inspirational incident of an amazing lady who only spoke from the Holy Qur'an throughout her life. We will leave it to our readers to marvel at her intelligence, knowledge and piety expressed in this breath-taking episode.
UK RRP:£3:00

Dearest Act to Allāh
Today our Masājid have lofty structures, engraved brickworks, exquisite chandeliers and laid rugs, but they are spiritually deprived due to the reason that the Masājid are used for social purposes including backbiting and futile talk rather than the performance of Salāh, Qur'ān recitation and the spreading of true authentic Islamic knowledge. This book elaborates on the etiquettes of the Masjid and the importance of Salāh with Quranic and prophetic proofs along with some useful anecdotes to emphasize their importance. **UK RRP:£3:00**

Don't Delay Your Nikāh
Marriage plays an important role in our lives. It is a commemoration of the union of two strangers who will spend the rest of their remaining lives with one another. Marriage ought to transpire comfort and tranquillity whereby the couple share one another's sorrow and happiness. It is strongly recommended that our brothers and sisters read and benefit from this book and try to implement it into our daily lives in order to once more revive the Sunnah of the Holy Prophet ﷺ on such occasions and repel the prevalent sins and baseless customs.
UK RRP:£3:00

Miracle of the Holy Qur'ān
The scholars of Islām are trying to wake us all up, however, we are busy dreaming of the present world and have forgotten our real destination. Shaykh Mufti Saiful Islām Sāhib has been conducted Tafsīr of the Holy Qur'ān every week for almost two decades with the purpose of reviving its teachings and importance. This book is a transcription of two titles; Miracle of the Holy Qur'ān and The Revelation of the Holy Qur'ān, both delivered during the weekly Tafsīr sessions.
UK RRP:£3:00

You are what you Eat
Eating Halāl and earning a lawful income plays a vital role in the acceptance of all our Ibādāt (worship) and good deeds. Mufti Saiful Islām Sāhib has presented a discourse on this matter in one of his talks. I found the discourse to be very beneficial, informative and enlightening on the subject of Halāl and Harām that clarifies its importance and status in Islām. I strongly recommend my Muslim brothers and sisters to read this treatise and to study it thoroughly.
UK RRP:£3:00